BAKELITE IN THE KITCHEN

Revised & Expanded 2nd Edition

Barbara E. Mauzy

Schiffer Publishing Ltd

4880 Lower Valley Road, Atglen, PA 19310 USA

DEDICATION

This book is lovingly dedicated to my mother, Patricia M. Schwartz. You gave me an eye to appreciate beauty and taught me to love books. Thanks!

Revised price guide: 2001
Copyright © 1998 & 2001 by Barbara Mauzy
Library of Congress Control Number: 2001091170

Designed by Sue
Typeset in Geometric 231 Heavy BT/Garamond

ISBN: 0-7643-1379-7
Printed in China
1 2 3 4

Published by Schiffer Publishing Ltd.
4880 Lower Valley Road
Atglen, PA 19310
Phone: (610) 593-1777; Fax: (610) 593-2002
E-mail: Schifferbk@aol.com
Please visit our web site catalog at
www.schifferbooks.com

This book may be purchased from the publisher.
Include $3.95 for shipping. Please try your bookstore first.
We are always looking for people to write books on new and related subjects. If you have an idea for a book please contact us at the above address.
You may write for a free catalog.

In Europe, Schiffer books are distributed by
Bushwood Books
6 Marksbury Avenue
Kew Gardens
Surrey TW9 4JF England
Phone: 44 (0) 20-8392-8585; Fax: 44 (0) 20-8392-9876
E-mail: Bushwd@aol.com
Free postage in the UK. Europe: air mail at cost.

CONTENTS

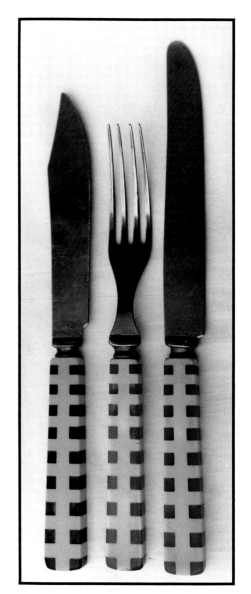

ACKNOWLEDGMENTS

Another year has gone by and my wonderful, understanding husband has endured this, my third book. Thanks to you, Jimmy Mike, for graciously tolerating the days and nights when Bakelite was piled everywhere. And thank you for the countless hours you stood patiently in the basement polishing piece, after piece, after piece…

I **MUST** offer the sincerest thanks to some people who helped to create this book. Thanks to Tom Donlan-Americana Factory for the napkin holder. I can always count on you for finding all kinds of unique pieces. Thank you Linda Karas/Polka Dots and Moonbeams for allowing me to interrupt your customers during a very busy antique show to take pictures of your wonderful merchandise. You were gracious and kind to a total stranger. A huge thank you with a long distance hug to Sally and Herbie Loeb. Although we have never met I feel bonded to you through this project. Your napkin rings really make this book complete. All of your other fabulous pieces you unselfishly photographed and shared will be appreciated by anyone looking through these pages. Thanks to Abby Nash, Malabar Enterprises, Ithaca, New York for willingly sharing your inventory and photography, too. You always find such great pieces! How do you do it? Thank you, thank you, thank you Penny Van Wart/ Peter Jones-Penny Toys. Your friendship and expertise means so much. You will see how much of you and your fabulous merchandise is poured all through this book. I appreciate all the direction, "stuff," and advice you generously offered. Many other unnamed people gave their time and energy to assist me. Thank you! Finally, I would be remiss to neglect Dot (Dorothy) and John D'Amour who have been a superlative source of piece after piece of Bakelite. Your continual searching on my behalf is now being shared with everyone. Thanks to you both!

Thanks to you, the reader and collector. Your passion for Bakelite makes the efforts of all of these wonderful people meaningful!

INTRODUCTION

An Historical Prospective

Chemist Dr. Leo Hendrick Baekeland developed and named Bakelite originally to be an insulator for electricity. Prior to Baekeland's discovery, chemists researching plastics formulated acids in shellac substitutes. Instead he used a base, ammonia, which insured final hardening and greatly reduced the gas content of the solution. His predecessors used temperatures in the 50-75 degree Celsius range, Baekeland went to temperatures of 150-200 degrees Celsius and added pressure. He discovered the more heat used the harder the substance became, and the birth of Bakelite occurred in his Yonkers, New York, laboratory in 1907.

Bakelite became an incredibly useful material because it was able to be laminated, stretched into fibers, and molded. By 1927 scientists had adapted it to dozens of applications, and Bakelite was on the brink of entering the "modern" kitchen. It was in 1927 that the concept of color in the kitchen was born, and Bakelite was a wonderful alternative to wood and metal because it was available in yellow, gold, white, cobalt blue, green, orange, red, brown, and black.

Community Plate (Oneida Community, Ltd) began to actively promote Bakelite-handled utensils in 1929, and magazines and catalogues show Bakelite-handled gadgets in kitchen scenes through the early 1950s. It was most popular during the 1930s and 1940s.

A cooking article in the March 1941 The American Home shows the table set with Bakelite-handled utensils.

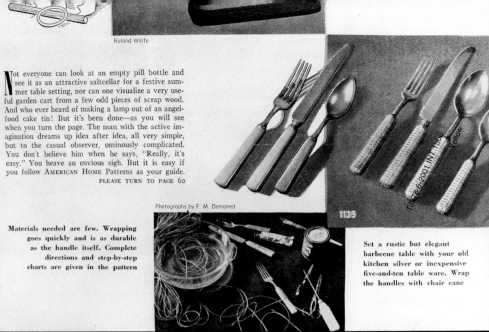

Roland Wolfe

Not everyone can look at an empty pill bottle and see it as an attractive saltcellar for a festive summer table setting, nor can one visualize a very useful garden cart from a few odd pieces of scrap wood. And who ever heard of making a lamp out of an angelfood cake tin! But it's been done—as you will see when you turn the page. The man with the active imagination dreams up idea after idea, all very simple, but to the casual observer, ominously complicated. You don't believe him when he says, "Really, it's easy." You heave an envious sigh. But it is easy if you follow AMERICAN HOME Patterns as your guide.
PLEASE TURN TO PAGE 60

Photographs by F. M. Demarest

Materials needed are few. Wrapping goes quickly and is as durable as the handle itself. Complete directions and step-by-step charts are given in the pattern

Set a rustic but elegant barbecue table with your old kitchen silver or inexpensive five-and-ten table ware. Wrap the handles with chair cane

On this buffet table are some interesting forks and knives with handles that appear to be woven. A June 1949 article in *The American Home* provides instruction on the technique. The message here is that the Bakelite-handle flatware in the reader's kitchen is now outdated so cover it up!

It is difficult to locate Bakelite in advertisements after 1951. *The American Home*, July 1951, showed red-handled utensils on a festive tablecloth. This is one of the most recent examples I was able to document.

DOROTHY LAMBERT TRUMM

Summer Linens

● Wilt-proof linens that won't wilt you in the making. These fresh new designs are easy to do with our painting patterns, go so quickly that they're finished before you know it! They cost so little (25¢ per pattern, plus your material), you can afford to make some. for different occasions. Try inexpensive unbleached muslin, Indianhead, cotton crash, or rayon. For more elegant settings, use linen. Or you could use these designs for tablecloths. Hem or fringe ends or all four sides. For gay and casual note our swaggering rooster boldly aping Ferdinand and his flowers, with the plate done in reverse colors. Little wooden horse, just over from Sweden, cheers you with his "Skål." Do a casserole, too, with ovenproof paint. Is fishing your hobby? An angelfish for you, plus another design of goblets and decanters. Or perhaps you prefer neat geometrics to grace your table or modern designs to play up plain color china. Whatever design you choose, it's fun!

Collecting Bakelite Kitchen Pieces

I am a firm believer that if an item gives you pleasure then no more needs to be said! Bakelite has a richness in its colors, forms, and textures. Kitchen pieces using Bakelite handles, knobs, or embellishments ask to be touched and used. So, I advise collectors to buy what they like and set an eclectic table. Utensils don't have to match, and colors don't have to be the same unless that is the look desired.

For collectors willing to buy piece-by-piece, whether matching handles or just purchasing items that appeal, the savings will be significant. The greater the set, be it flatware or cooking gadgets, the higher the price. Finding Bakelite treasures one at a time will usually save money, but the trade-off is the time one must take if building a set is a goal. A service of flatware for twelve will cost significantly more than two exact sets of six. If a collector wants a service for twelve **grab it** because these are few and far between. However, twelve different place settings creates an interesting and colorful table that only Bakelite can provide. There's no right or wrong, so allow creativity to reign!

Handle Styles

It doesn't matter what styles are the most popular among other collectors, what matters is what appeals to YOU! Some people don't like the look of white plastic between the metal and Bakelite on flatware.

They might pass on these pieces. Yet others look at the interesting handle design and good quality of the stainless steel and rejoice that there are spoons while they scoop up a pleasing grouping. Collectors' tastes are as varied as the individuals themselves. Buy what you like!

There are a few handles I need to clarify here to make using this book easy.

These kitchen gadgets have "BULLET" handles made by Androck.

The yellow "V" design in these handles is a "CHEV-RON." It was made by laminating a contrasting color of Bakelite within a handle. These pieces are difficult to find, and they will cost significantly more than single-colored handles.

Indentifying Bakelite Pieces

The best technique for determining whether or not a piece of plastic is Bakelite is the thumb-rubbing test. First rub your thumb on a piece of fabric such as your sleeve. This removes other scents and your own oils. Then vigorously rub the surface of the item while applying some pressure thus creating friction. When your thumb is hot stop and sniff both the item in question and your thumb. If you detect a "rubbery" odor VOILA! You have Bakelite. This is not always one hundred percent accurate. Sometimes it seems impossible to create an odor, but this is the best, most portable method I know.

If you're still uncertain as to the material of an item even after the thumb-rubbing test, ask some questions. As with any purchase you as a collector are considering, know your dealer. Buy from a reputable, informed individual who can answer your questions. You also owe it to yourself to be informed. Hopefully this book will provide knowledge and guidance for consumers and dealers alike.

The question of Bakelite, Catalin, Marbalin, and Lucite may initially pose some confusion. It is really simple. Bakelite was made by Baekeland's company beginning in 1910. Lucite was invented in 1930. It is distinguishable by its transparency, even if colored. The Catalin Corporation, also a producer of plastics, purchased patents in 1932 that allowed them to produce a material chemically the same as Bakelite, but they marketed it as Catalin, and Marbalin is still another name for this same phenol resin. Bakelite, Catalin, Marbalin, call it what you wish, just call it fun to collect and wonderful to have.

Sometimes it is easy to determine the manufacturer of a given piece.

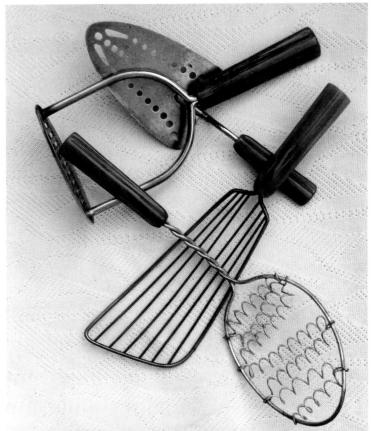

The blade of this knife clearly shows the name "Washington Forge." When possible, I provided manufacturer information for the pieces presented in this book.

Many (maybe even most!) gadgets were unmarked. Sometimes "Stainless Steel" or "U.S.A." were the only identifying words placed on an item.

These four kitchen gadgets have the same handle style. One can assume that they have the same manufacturer. Assume is all one can do because there are no manufacturer names on these pieces.

Even finding an original, unused boxed set may be of no help in determining the manufacturer. These four gadgets **and the box** are unmarked.

Eventually one can acquire enough pieces with the same handle design and a name may appear on one, thus identifying the lot. However, that is not true in this case.

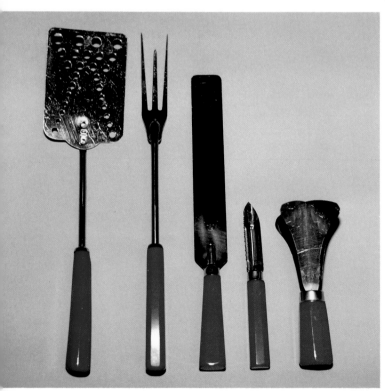

The following list represents manufacturers of kitchenware cited in this book. They didn't necessarily manufacture the Bakelite, but they used the material in some way, usually as a handle.

A & J
A & J EKCO
Androck
B.K. Company
Bates
Boker
Blue Whirl
Burns Manufacturing Company
Cayuga
CHEES-SERVE Manufacturing Company
Clear Cryst
D & S
DS
Durever
Edlund Company
EKCO
Eagle Precision Manufacturing Corporation
Englishtown Cutlery Limited
EVERBRITE
Federal
FIRTH
G.S.C. Company
General Cutlery Company
Hampshire
Henry's (Henry Fox)
HOLCO (August W. Holmberg Company)
HULL
Imperial
Justinus
KROMEBRITE
Landers
Marvel
Megheny Forge
MOLLY PITCHER QUALITY CUTLERY
Monroe Silver Company
N.S.O. PERMA-BRITE
N.S.Company
NICHT ROSTEND GRANTON
PEERLESS
PERMA-BRITE
REGENT
Rival Manufacturing Company
Robinson Knife Company
ROESTVRIJ
ROSTFREI SOLINGEN
ROYAL BRAND CUTLERY COMPANY
C.J. Schneider Manufacturing Company
SHARPCUTTER

Sheffield
Shore Craft
Shur Edged
Specialty Guild Incorporated
STA-BRITE
STA-BRITE ALLEGHENY
Stanley Home Products
Universal (Landers, Frary & Clark)
Valley Forge
Vaughan
VOOS
Washington Forge
Wizard
WORLBEATER

Why is this homemaker from 1947 (*The American Home*, June) smiling? Because of her towels? Maybe. Or maybe it's the joy of using and displaying her lively Bakelite utensils! They all match, but yours don't have to.

Caring For Your Bakelite

Here are my three rules to follow to protect your Bakelite pieces and still enjoy using them:

1. Avoid extreme heat sources (like the coils of an electric stove) as Bakelite can burn and melt.
2. Wash by hand. Do not ever put Bakelite in a dishwasher. The harsh detergents and high heat can dry out the Bakelite (to the point of cracking) and dull the vivid colors.
3. Allow yourself the pleasure of really using your pieces.

A Note From the Author

Assessing values to anything is quite difficult. A friend sat with me at an auction. After vigorous bidding on an item she turned to me and said, "So that's what it's worth." "No," I replied, "that's what someone was willing to pay." Neither the publisher or the author are responsible for any financial loss or gain due to the values assigned in this book. My intent is to provide a guide. As a teacher I feel very strongly that consumers need to be educated. I have attempted to do that with this book, and the pricing here is provided to assist, not dictate. What something is worth is truly up to the seller and the buyer.

I hope you, dear reader, derive as much pleasure from reading this book as I have had in building it. I love Bakelite, and yes, I do collect it!

CHAPTER 1: PREPARING THE FOOD

Beaters

A variety of beater styles are available with Bakelite handles. The value of a given beater is determined by the uniqueness of the piece as well as creative use of color. A beater with an uncommon configuration or with multiple colors will have a higher value.

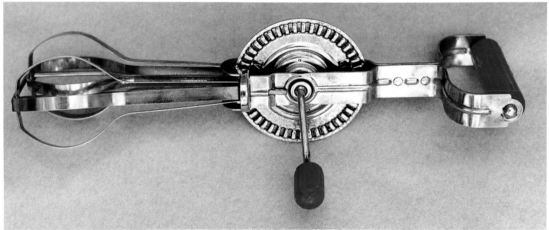

These, the most common styles and colors of beaters, are worth $20-$30 apiece.
Black & red: Androck with ribs to accompany bullet-handled pieces, 1941
Maroon: A&J EKCO Products Company
Red with "T" handle: Androck, 1930
Light green: Hi-speed EKCO Beater
Dark green: Edlund Company, 1931
Yellow: Hi-Speed A&J Beater

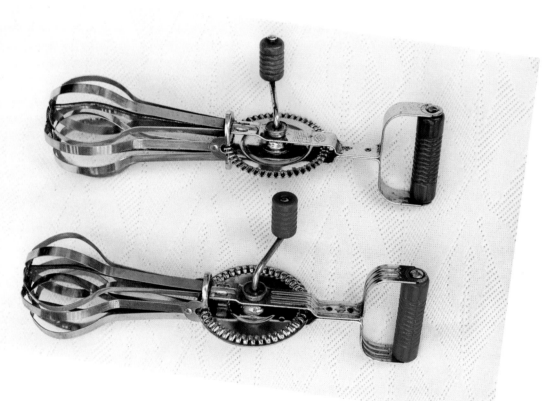

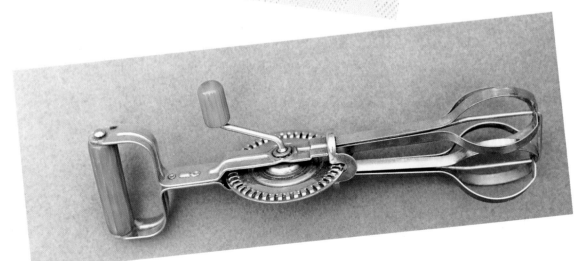

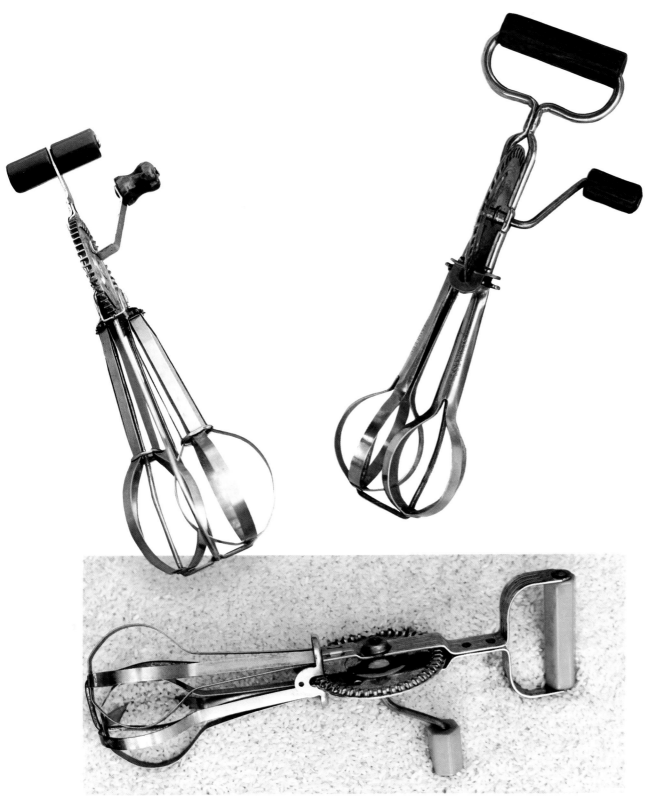

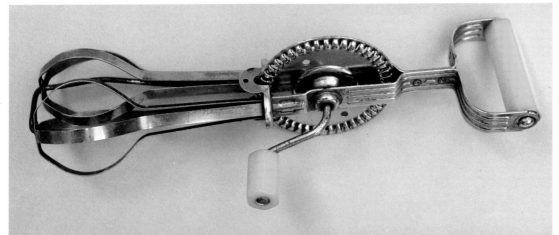

Uncommon handle treatment and design make these beaters worth $50-60 each. "One-Hand Wip" Eagle Precision Mfg Corp. New York, one squeeze turns the beater heads two complete rotations Red & butterscotch: Blue Whirl

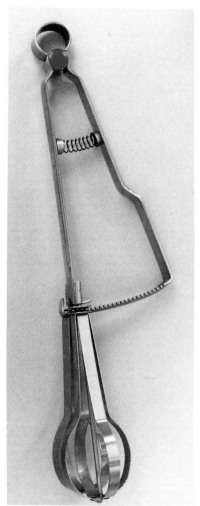

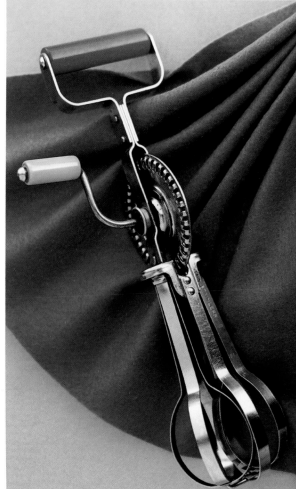

$65-$75 each
Tri-colored: EKCO Prod. Co.
Yellow: WORLBEATER, Los Angeles, Cal.

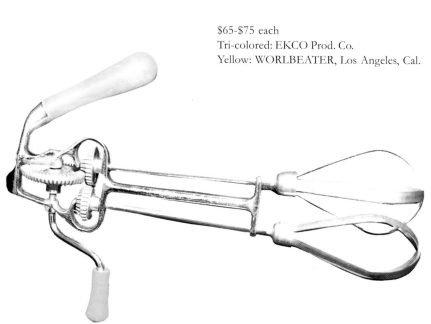

16

This Rival Speed Mixer originally sold for $9.95 and is now worth $90-$100 as shown with all of its attachments. Rival Manufacturing Company, Kansas City, Missouri, 1943

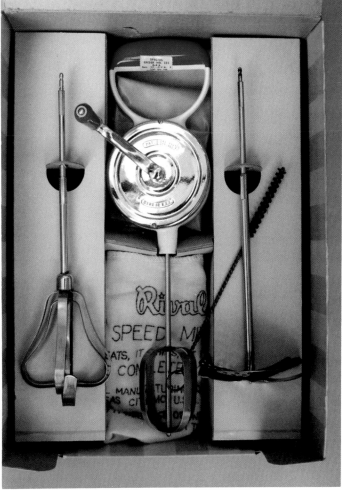

Choppers

All of the choppers shown have multiple blades for reducing food items. The condition of the blades is as important as the integrity of the Bakelite handles.

Any one of these choppers is worth $20-$30 apiece.
Black & red: Androck with ribs to accompany bullet-handled pieces
Red with cylindrical handle: A&J
Greens: all unmarked

Cleavers

Despite the difficulty one might have in locating Bakelite cleavers they are not particularly popular. Their elusiveness does not add to their collectiblity or value.

$30-35 each

Corn Creamers

Triangular edges create a cutting implement for preparing creamed corn.

$20-25 apiece

Dough Blenders

Handle shape and color are the only differences among various dough blenders.

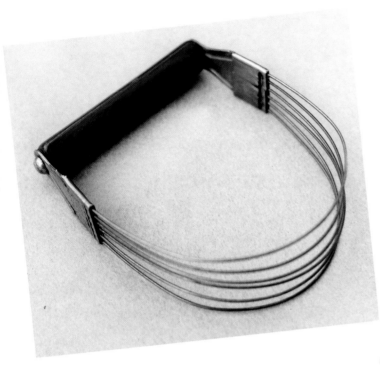

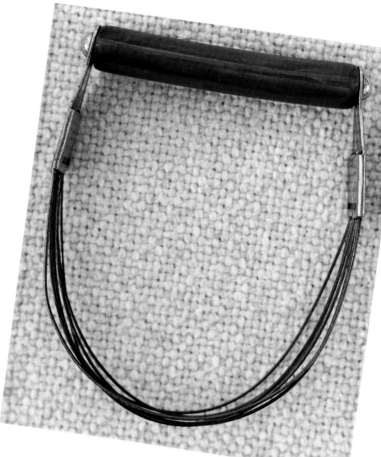

Two views of an Androck dough blender reveal a patent date of 11-12-29.

Expect to pay $20-$28 for a dough blender. All of these examples are Androck. The red and yellow Bakelite handles are ribbed to accompany bullet-handled utensils.

Garnishing Tools

Pictured are coring tools, peelers, and melon ball makers.

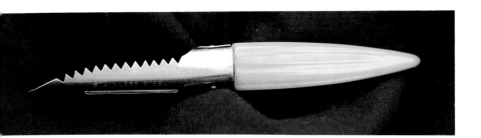

$20-25 each
Gold: 1925
Red: Wizard brand
Yellow and red bullet handles: Androck
Peeler: Made in U.S.A.
Melon ball makers: unmarked

Graters

These stainless steel and Bakelite graters are just more than 9 inches in length.

$15-$18 apiece

Knife Sharpeners

A variety of knife sharpener designs are presented. Note the tremendous difference in value reflected in the unusual pieces.

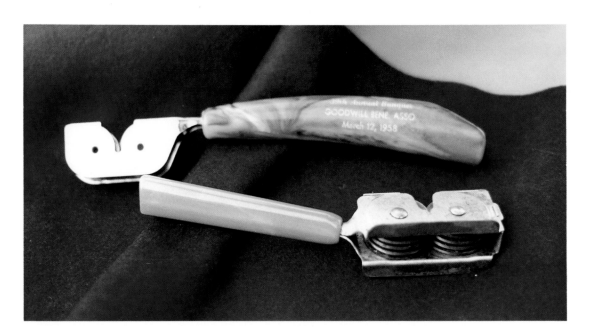

$20-$25 each
Marbled: March 12, 1958
Gold: A&J

RARE! $75-$85

RARE! The HOLCO "JUNIOR" originally sold for $4 and is now worth $80-$90.

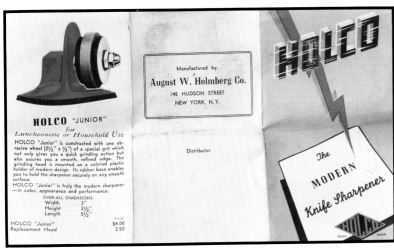

23

Meat Lifters

Meat lifters measure about 8.5 inches and may be difficult to find.

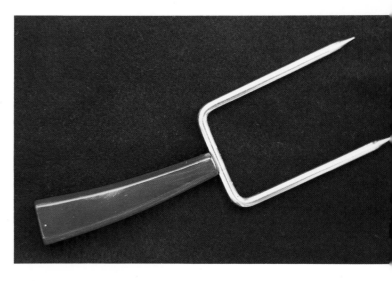

Red, $25-$30; brown $15-$18

Meat Saws

This is the only example of a meat saw I was able to locate.

1964, $15-18

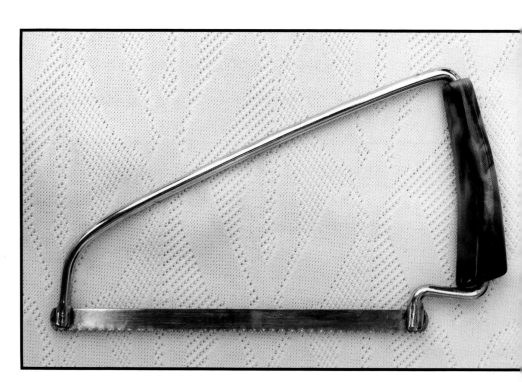

Meat Tenderizers

At 6.75 inches, this is the only meat tenderizer I was able to find.

A patent from 1965 is on this tenderizer that would sell for $12-$15.

Openers

One-piece openers have a lower value than those that separate into two pieces unless the handle is both Bakelite and Lucite. Advertising may add interest to openers, but the real value is in the design and handle treatment.

Brown, $8-$10; green, $15-$20

This jar opener would cost a collector $18-20.

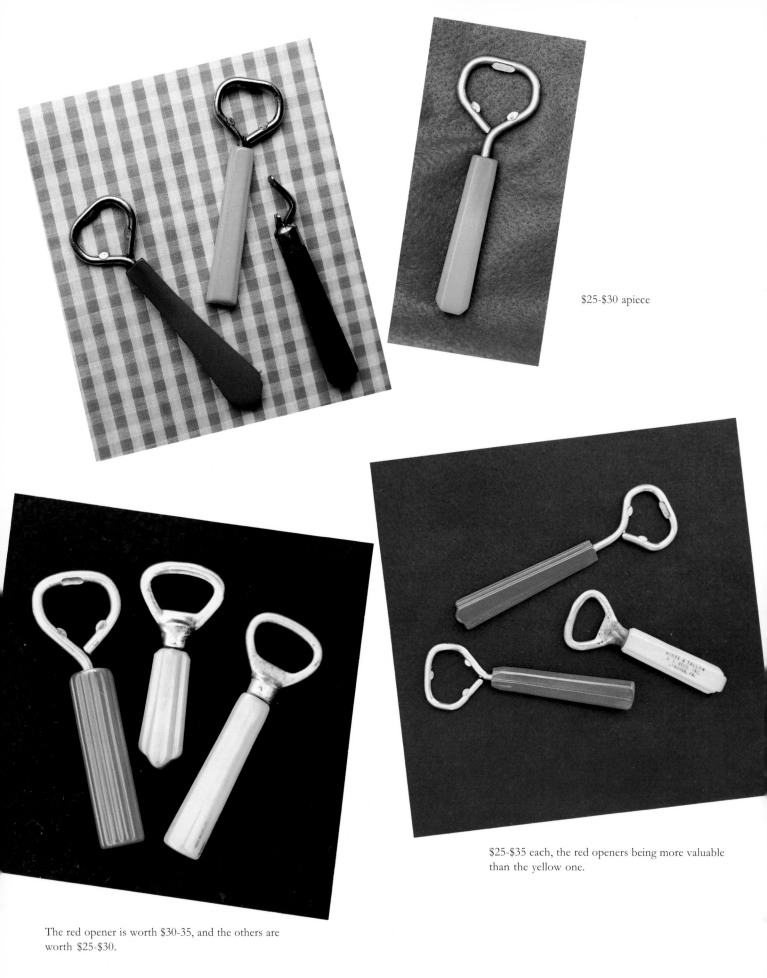

$25-$30 apiece

$25-$35 each, the red openers being more valuable than the yellow one.

The red opener is worth $30-35, and the others are worth $25-$30.

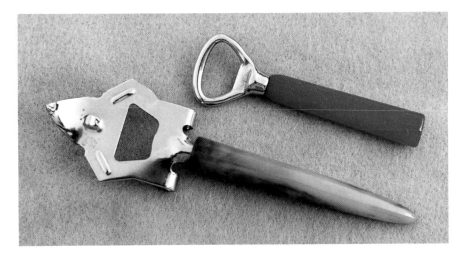

Brown $20-$25 Red $30-$35

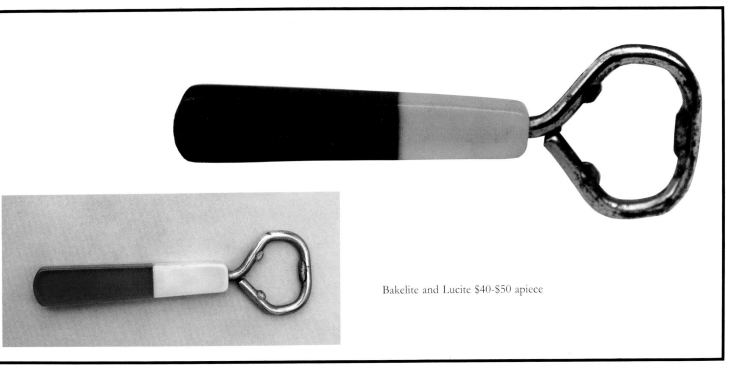

Bakelite and Lucite $40-$50 apiece

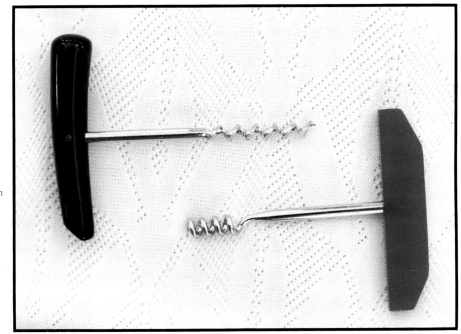

$25-$30 each

27

The one-piece red opener is worth $25-$30 and the others are $40-$50.

Pie Crimpers

Pie crimpers are a most elusive kitchen item. The all-Bakelite examples are almost impossible to find.

Two views of Vaughan's Pie Trimmer & Sealer $30-$40

Smaller crimper $100-$120, Larger crimper $125-$150

Potato Mashers

Potato mashers are popular even with those kitchen collectors who are decorating predominately in wooden-handled gadgets. They are functional, easy to display, and readily available in the marketplace.

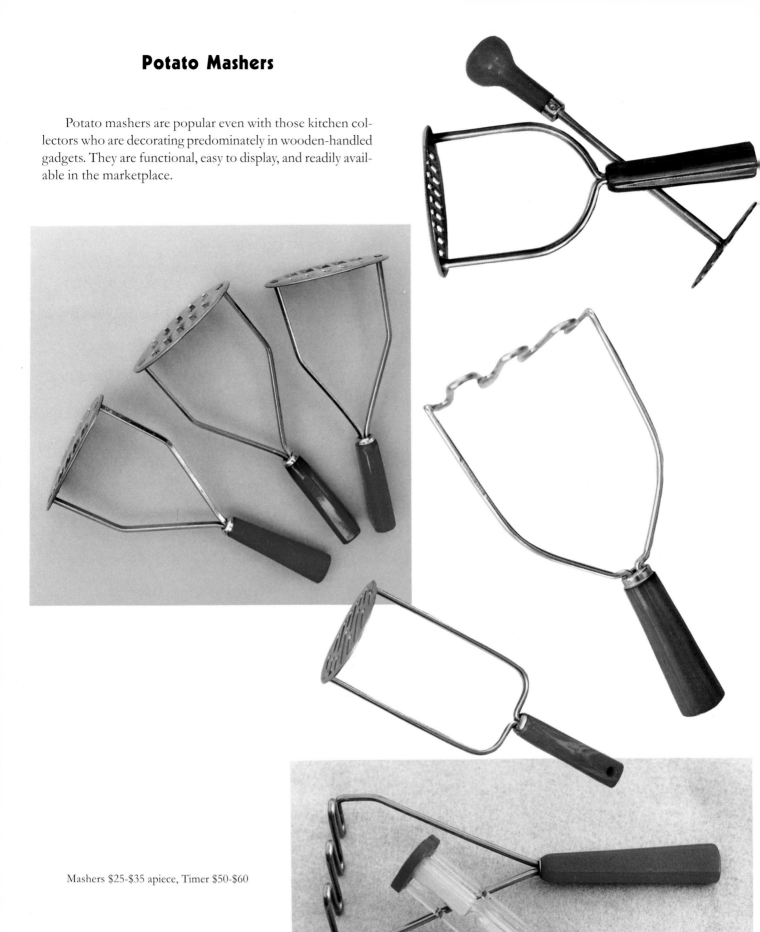

Mashers $25-$35 apiece, Timer $50-$60

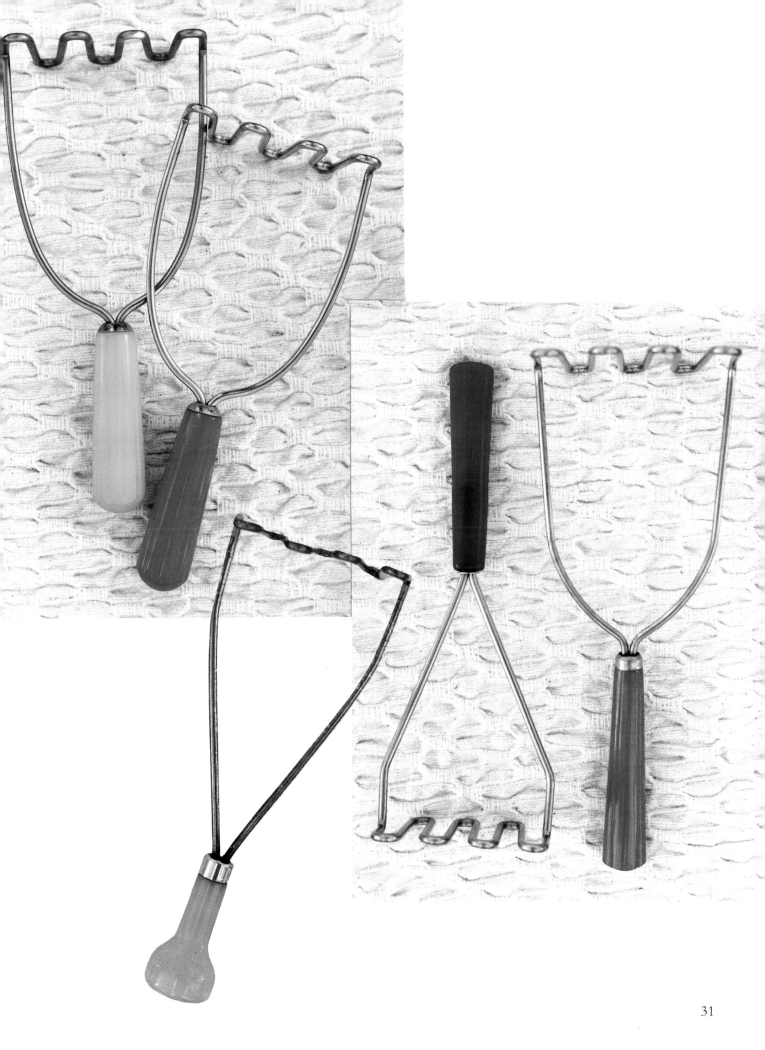

Scoops

Shown are two "LEVEL FULL ¼ CUP" scoops designed for dry measuring in two different handle designs. These A&J gadgets are extremely popular with collectors. The green handle is marbled or swirled in the popular "end-of-the-day" look. Ice cream scoops are presented in the section "Serving the Meal."

$55-$65 ea.

Spatulas

Here are nine spatulas and two advertisements showing many of the different spatula variations.

Opposite page:
This advertisement from the January 1941 *Ladies' Home Journal* shows a black bullet-handled spatula.

Androck bullet-handled spatulas $30-$35 each

$25-$30 apiece

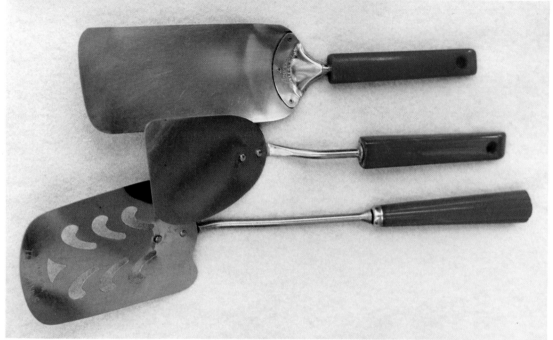

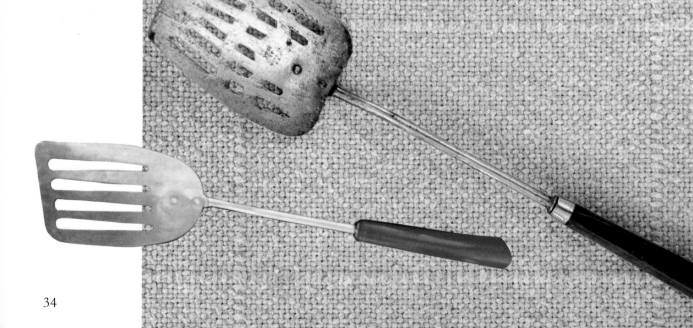

34

1. 3 minute sausage!

This is Swift's Premium Brown 'N Serve Sausage, ready quick as your breakfast eggs. Just brown 'n serve—and enjoy. Each lean link is fully cooked, practically no shrinkage. It comes ten to eleven links per package.

There's new convenience for you in these

5. Packaged Sandwich Steaks ready in minutes!
What's your pleasure? They're all tender-frozen, all lean beef, all Swift's Premium. Stock your freezer with four kinds: Ready Quick Beef Sandwich Steaks,

Loin Luncheon Steaks, Pure Beef Hamburger Patties and Buttered Chopped Beef Steaks. Loaded with protein, yet low in calories. Flavor sealed in new red and white aluminum foil packages. Look for them in your food store frozen food case.

This "Swift's Premium" advertisement shows a red Bakelite spatula.

Spreaders

Along with the spreaders are some butter knives and a pastry server. More butter knives are pictured in the "Knives" section of this book. Pastry servers are shown in greater detail in the "Pastry Server" section of "Serving the Meal."

Androck bullet handle $35-$40

Bottom left: *Left:* Unmarked spreader that is 11" long and 2.5" wide; *middle:* unmarked 12" spreader with stainless steel ring for hanging, *right:* unmarked 11.25" spreader; $20-$25 each.

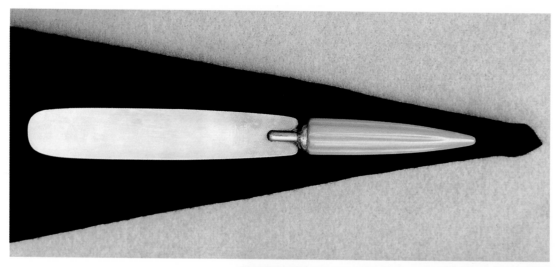

Androck bullet handle $30-$35

Middle (Androck bullet handle) $30-$35, others $20-$25 apiece

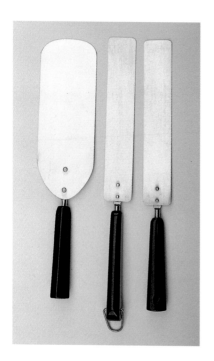

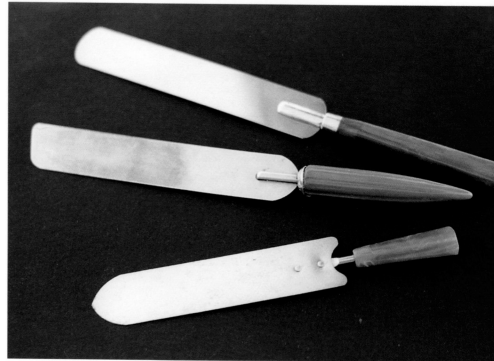

$20-$25 each
Yellow: Androck

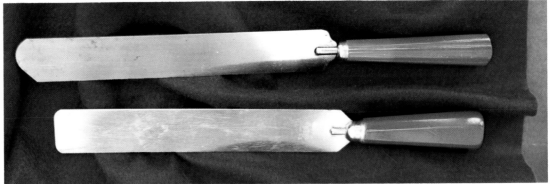

Butter knives $8-$10 apiece, spreader and pastry server $20-$25 apiece

Strainers

Larger-sized strainers or those with a bullet handle have a higher value than others. Also shown is a tea strainer complete with a small Bakelite knob at the end of its handle.

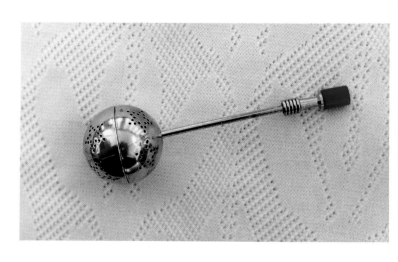

Tea strainer $50-$60

Larger size (5" across) Androck $30-$35 apiece

Smaller size (2.5" across) Androck $20-$25 each

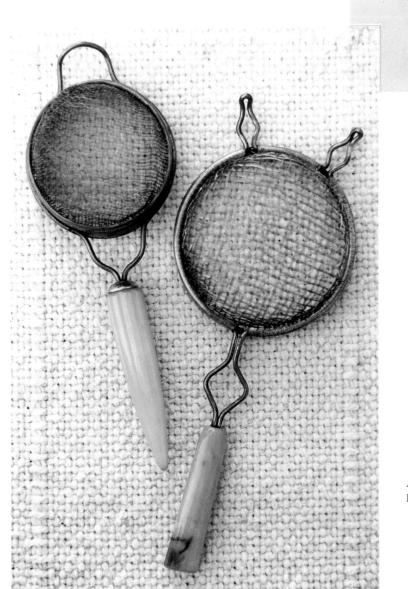

Androck bullet $20-$25, other A&J AJAX
Heavy Cloth Strainer $15-$20

$15-$20 apiece

Whips

Pricing for whips reflects rarity of design.

$20-$30 each

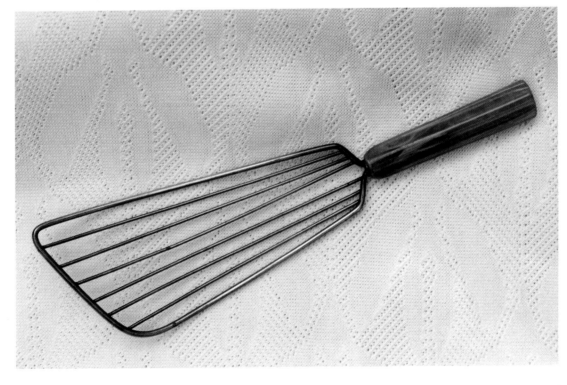

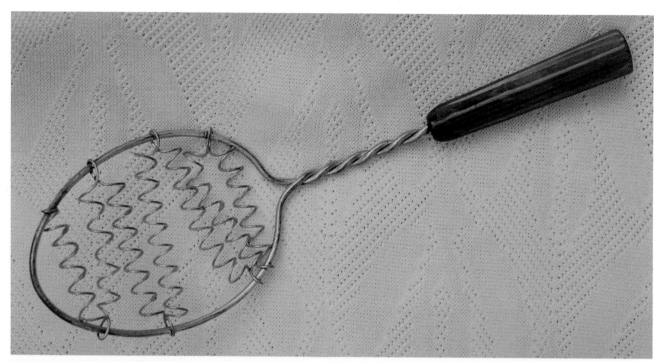

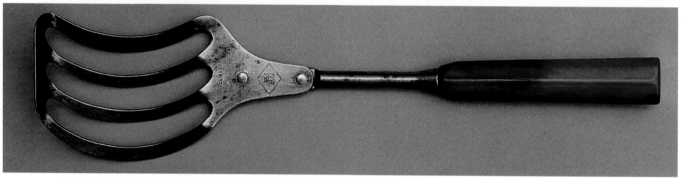

Top: $30-$35
Bottom: A&J $35-$45

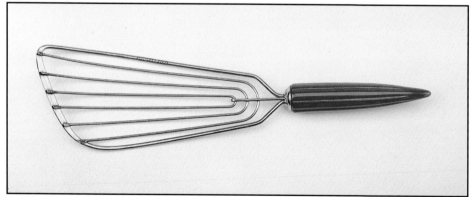

Androck bullet-handled whip in Stainless Steel, $25-$35.

9.25" A&J whip in an unusual style. Marked "PAT. APLD.FOR" $35-$45.

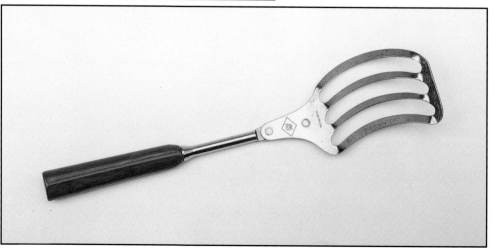

CHAPTER 2: SERVING THE MEAL

Cake-Breakers

These handy tools are also referred to as cake-cutters and angel food cutters. Basic in design, the only real difference between various cake-breakers is the handle treatment. An unusual handle will increase the value of a cake-breaker.

The paper insert from C.J. Schneider Mfg. Co. shows Cake-Breakers, CheeSliceRs, and KOB-KNOBS (corn holders). The Cake-Breaker has a patent number from 1932.

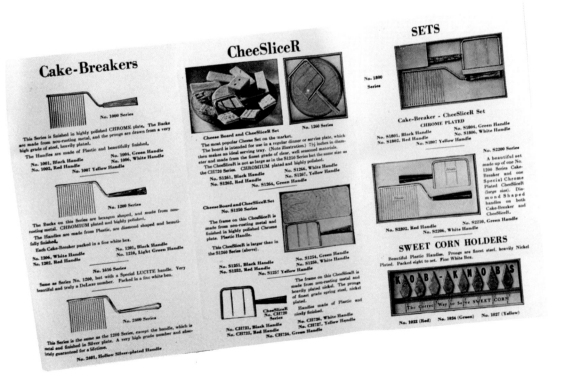

$15-$20 apiece

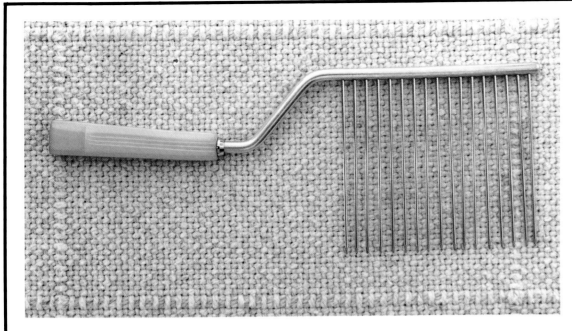

$20-$25 each

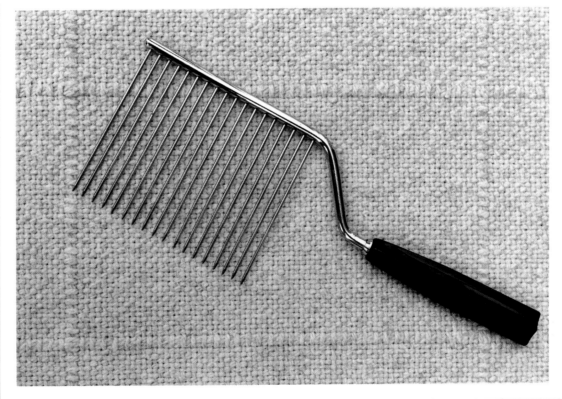

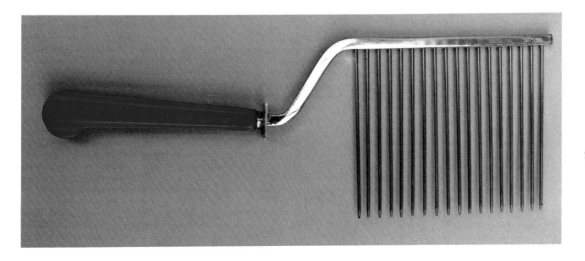

$25-$30

45

Carving Sets and Meat Forks

Carving sets typically had three pieces: a meat fork, a carving knife, and a sharpening steel. Some sets included individual steak knives. The last piece photographed for this section was designed to hold steady a large piece of meat when slicing. This is the only one of these I have ever seen. More knives are shown in "Handles! Handles! Handles!"

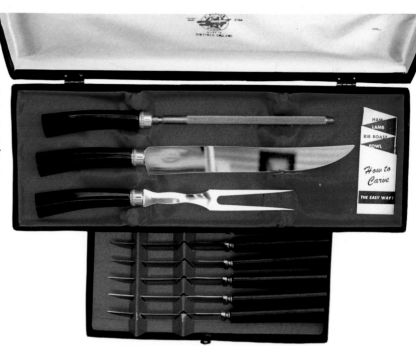

Complete carving sets in black Bakelite are difficult to locate. Sheffield Stainless Steel Blades Made in Sheffield, England, $100-$125

The close-up photograph shows an unusual handle on this boxed set from Sheffield, England. $85-$100

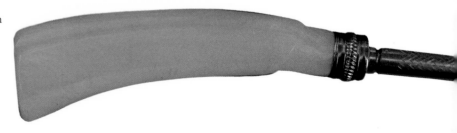

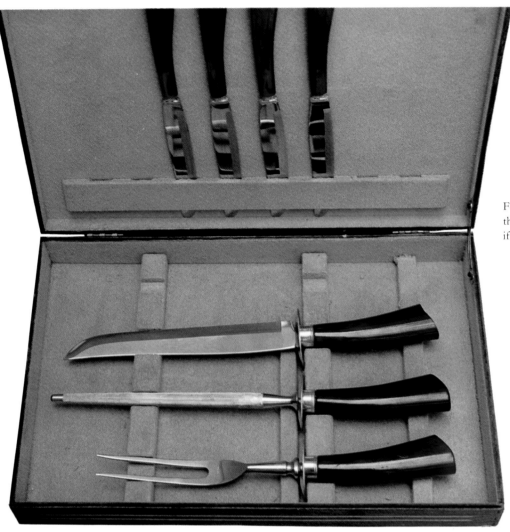

Four steak knives are missing in this Englishtown set. $100-$125 if complete

Carving sets often did not include individual steak knives.

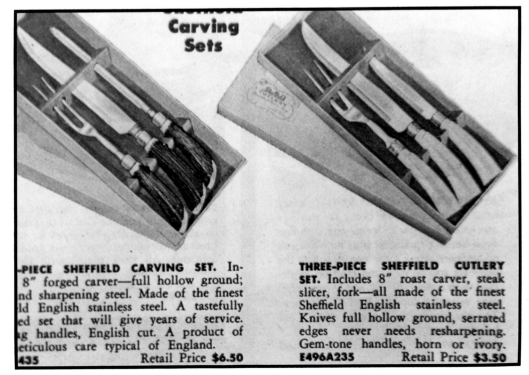

Carving Sets

-PIECE SHEFFIELD CARVING SET. In-
8″ forged carver—full hollow ground;
nd sharpening steel. Made of the finest
ld English stainless steel. A tastefully
ed set that will give years of service.
g handles, English cut. A product of
eticulous care typical of England.
435   Retail Price **$6.50**

**THREE-PIECE SHEFFIELD CUTLERY
SET.** Includes 8″ roast carver, steak
slicer, fork—all made of the finest
Sheffield English stainless steel.
Knives full hollow ground, serrated
edges never needs resharpening.
Gem-tone handles, horn or ivory.
E496A235   Retail Price **$3.50**

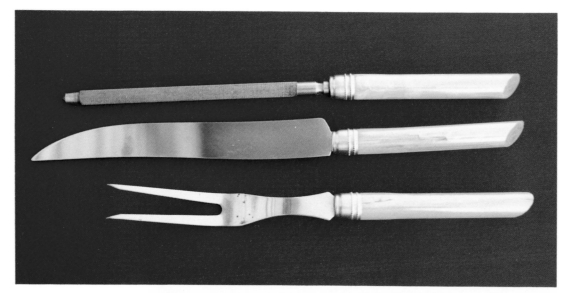

$40-$50 per set

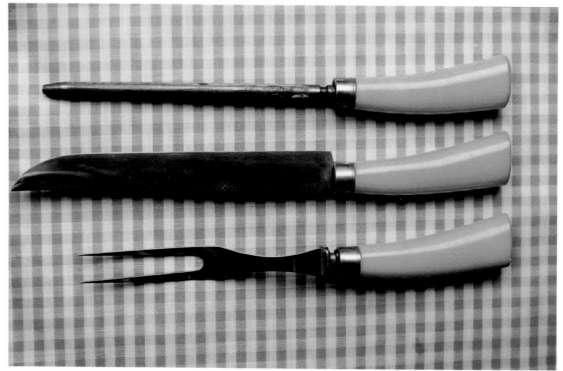

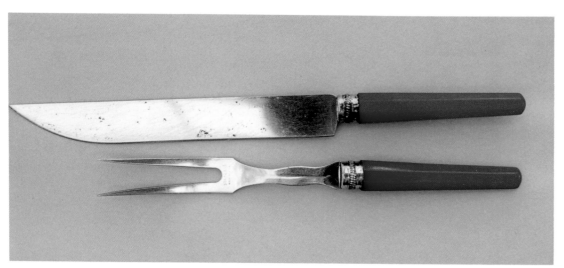

$35-$40

48

All three pieces have the same handle. $18-$22 for any single utensil

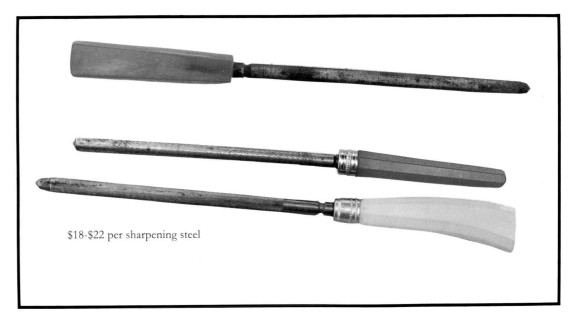

$18-$22 per sharpening steel

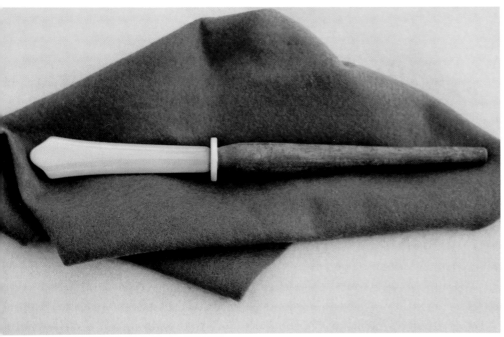

$25-$30 for this unusual handle treatment

Meat forks retail for $18-$22 each in these more common styles.

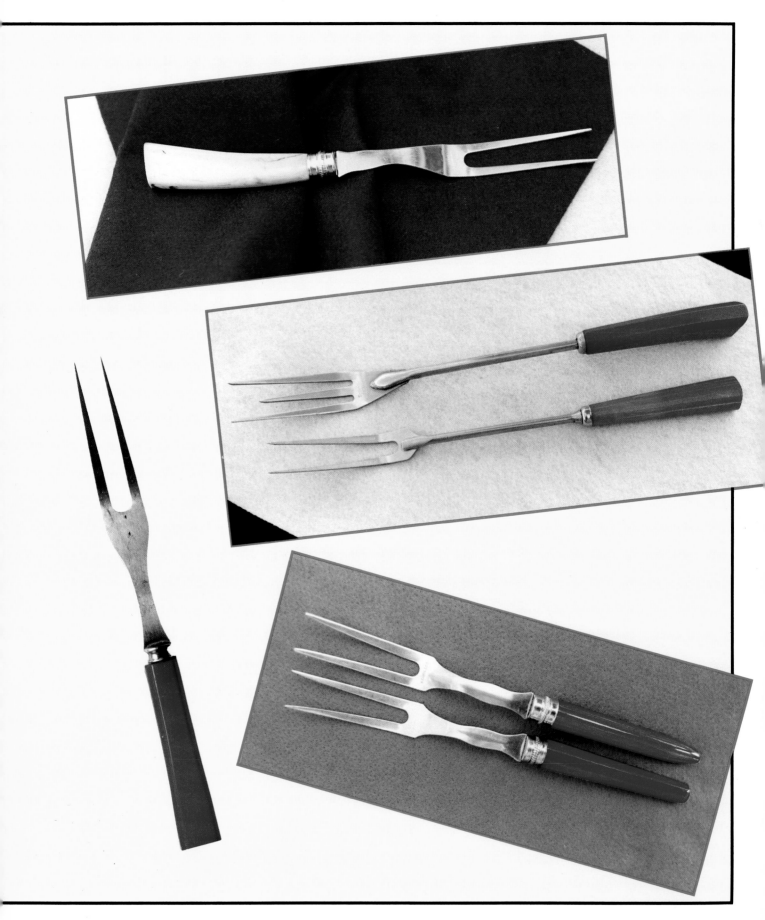

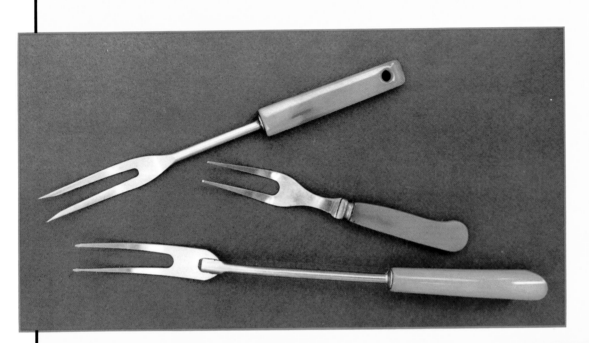

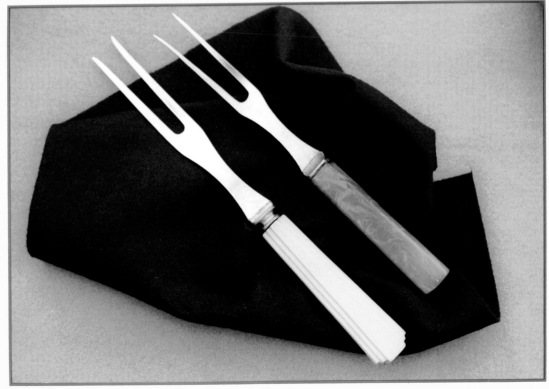

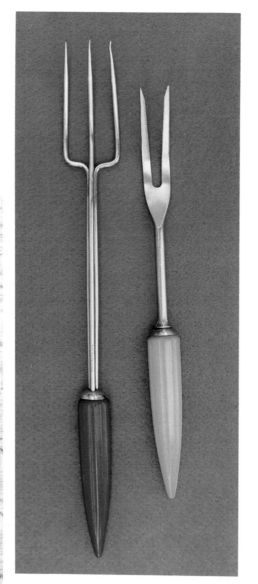

Androck bullet-handled forks command a higher price of $25-$30 apiece.

$30-$35

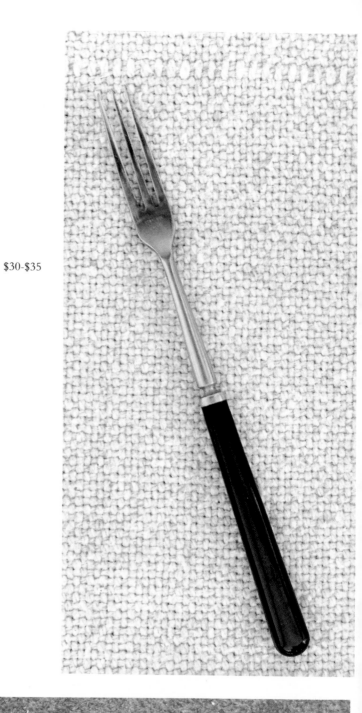

This meat holder is a truly special piece. $100-$110

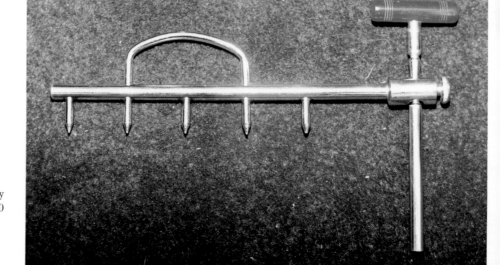

Cheese Slicers

Presented are four distinctly different kinds of cheese slicers. These clever gadgets perform their task effectively.

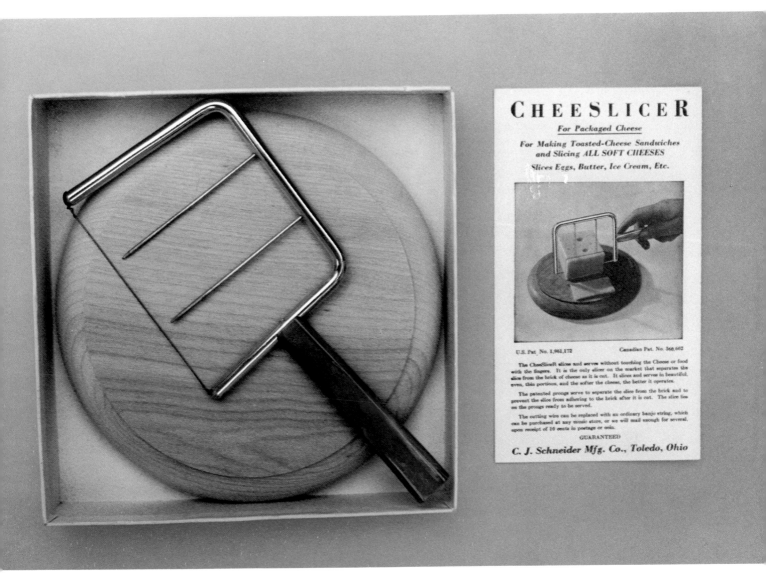

This C.J. Schneider Mfg. Co. "CheeSliceR" came boxed with a cutting board. The patent number is from 1934. $45-$60 complete with box and original paper directions

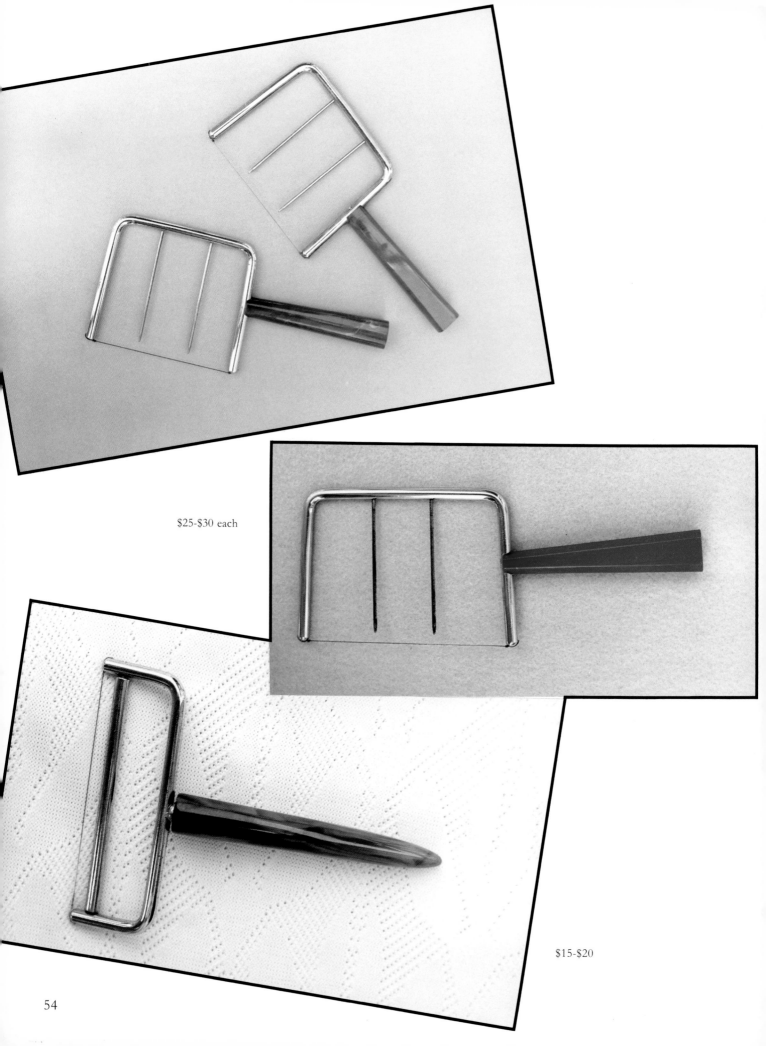

$25-$30 each

$15-$20

54

SLICE EASILY AND SERVE

Hostess
Cheese Slicer
AND SERVER

$20-$25 each

The PERFECT way to slice those hard-to-handle hard cheeses. The secret is in the pointed tines which serve as spreaders. Furnishes a wonderful cheese server, too.

LANGNER MFG. CO., NEW YORK 1, N. Y.

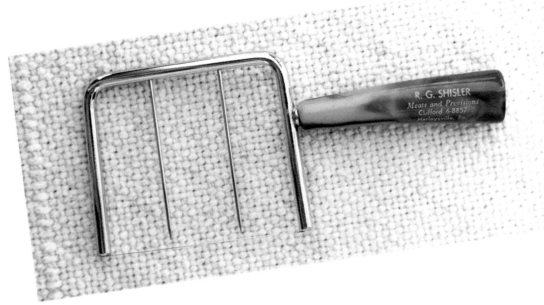

R. G. SHISLER
Meats and Provisions
Clifford 6-8857
Harleysville, Pa.

Cheese planes are difficult to find and therefore more costly.
$35-$45 apiece
Two-toned Bakelite: ROESTVRIJ
Red: Imperial

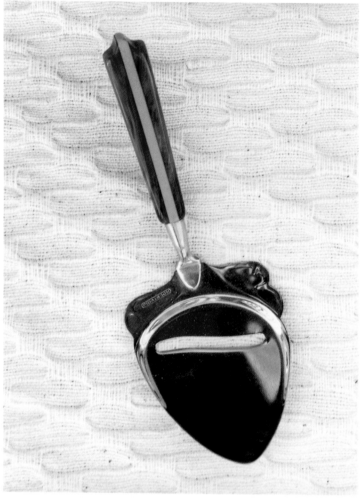

CHEESE SLICER AND SERVER
The Ideal Way to Slice and Serve
PACKAGE CHEESE

Move cutting bar to extreme right position. Place cheese on board near back edge. Bring cutting wire over cheese to desired thickness, wafer thin or half inch thick.

Also slices quarter sticks of butter.

To clean wipe with damp cloth.

CHEE-SERVE MFG. CO.

DETROIT   MICHIGAN

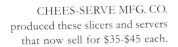

CHEES-SERVE MFG. CO. produced these slicers and servers that now sell for $35-$45 each.

Forks and Salad Sets

This section documents serving implements. Forks used for dining are located in the section "Setting the Table." As with other Bakelite utensils, the more unique pieces have a higher value than the common ones. Handles made with Bakelite and Lucite are premium pieces coveted by many collectors.

4.5 inches long, $30-$35

$10-$15

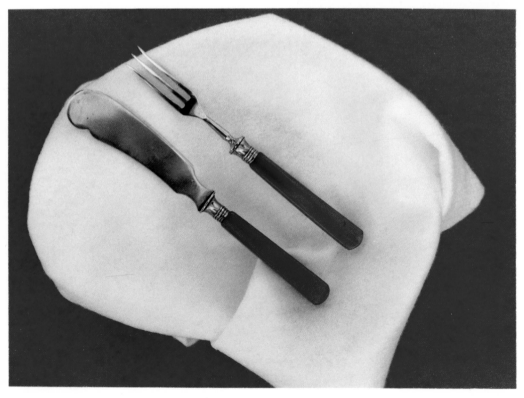

Orange Bakelite handles enhance the value of this set. $40-$50

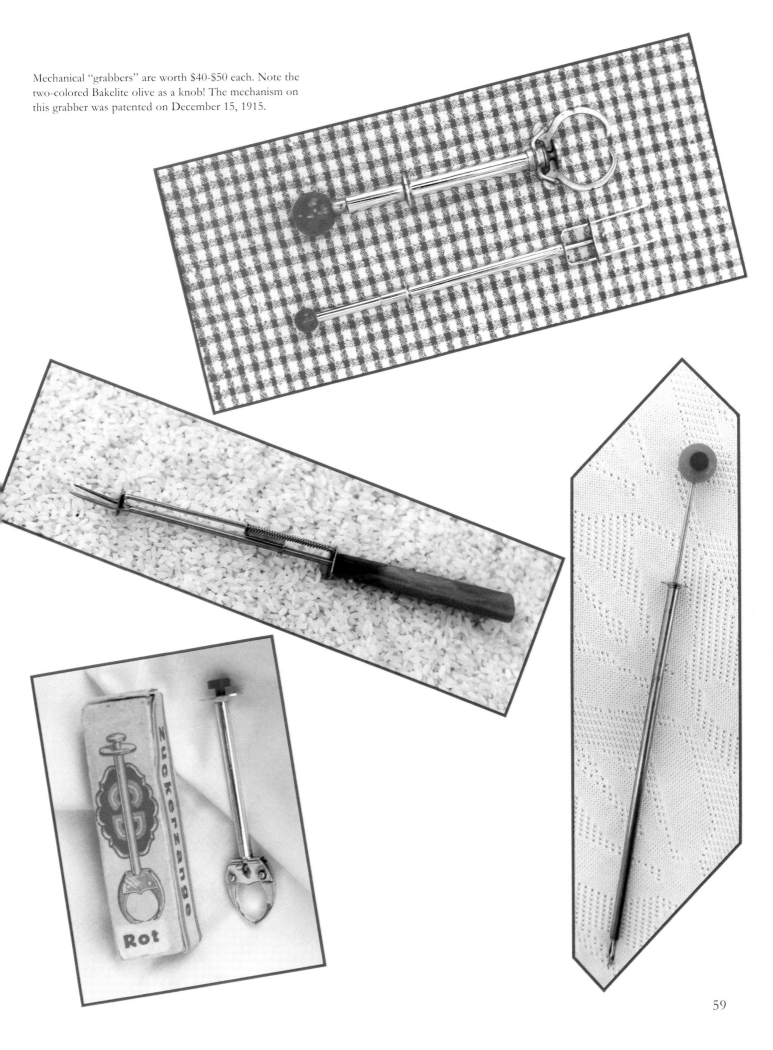

Mechanical "grabbers" are worth $40-$50 each. Note the two-colored Bakelite olive as a knob! The mechanism on this grabber was patented on December 15, 1915.

$10-$15 apiece

This salad fork is a commonly seen style worth $15-$20.

The handle on this PERMA-BRITE salad fork is popular among collectors. $35-$40

Due to the plainness of the Bakelite handle, the butterscotch salad fork is only worth $20-$25. KROMEBRITE's Bakelite and Lucite handled fork is worth $50-$60.

$50-$60 per set

$55-65 for the set

$15-$20 for the set

Ice Cream Scoops

Red Bakelite-handled ice cream scoops are the most common of any color. With luck a shopper may find them at price lower than listed here. Occasionally sellers confuse Bakelite handles with lower-priced plastic handles.

Black unmarked scoop 9 inches long $45-$55

Red "Maid of Honor" scoop 8 inches long $45-$55

Shore Craft 8 inches long $ 45-$55

Green Shore Craft scoop $50-$60

63

Ice Tongs

Ice tongs are no easy to find, particularly in good condition, as the prongs tend to be misshapen and the metal is often corroded.

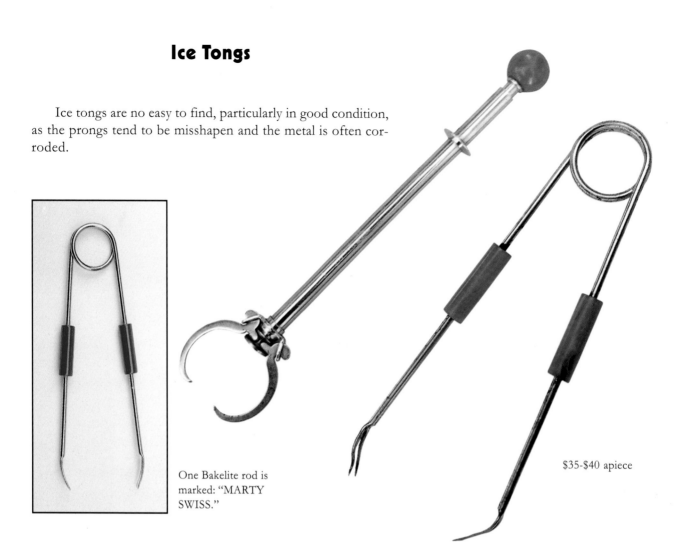

One Bakelite rod is marked: "MARTY SWISS."

$35-$40 apiece

Ladles

Ladles are among the most useful of all kitchen gadgets. One may no longer mash potatoes by hand or take the time to garnish a meal but serving meals often requires the use of a ladle. Care must be taken to not allow the Bakelite handle rest against a hot pot or cooking surface as the Bakelite may melt or burn.

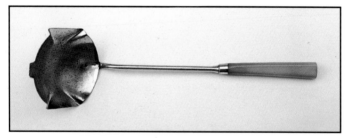

The design of this unmarked 13" ladle is perfect for either the right-handed or the left-handed chef. Although the bowl has wear, the uniqueness of this gadget makes it quite desirable. $30-$35.

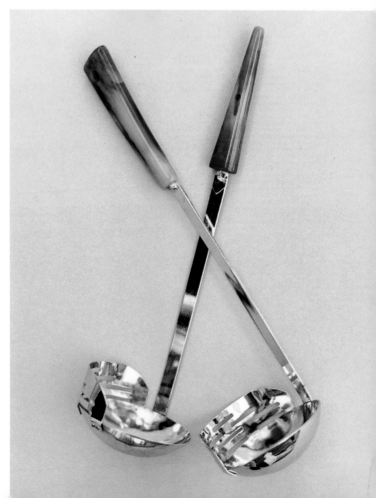

Both ladles have strainers on one side of their bowls. $25-$30 each

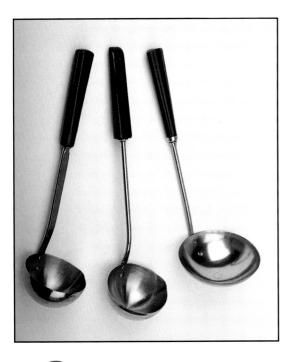

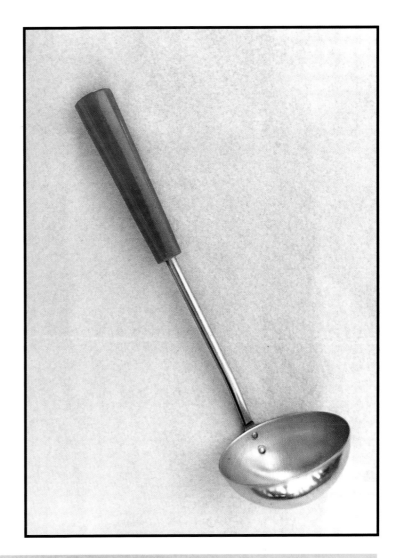

$25-$30 apiece

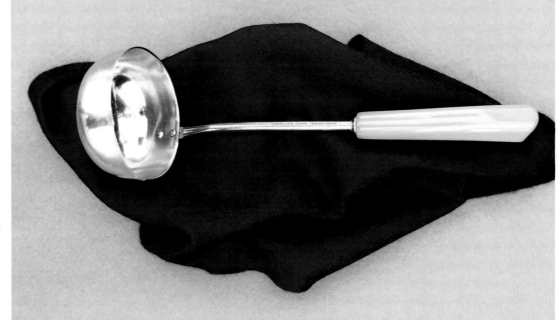

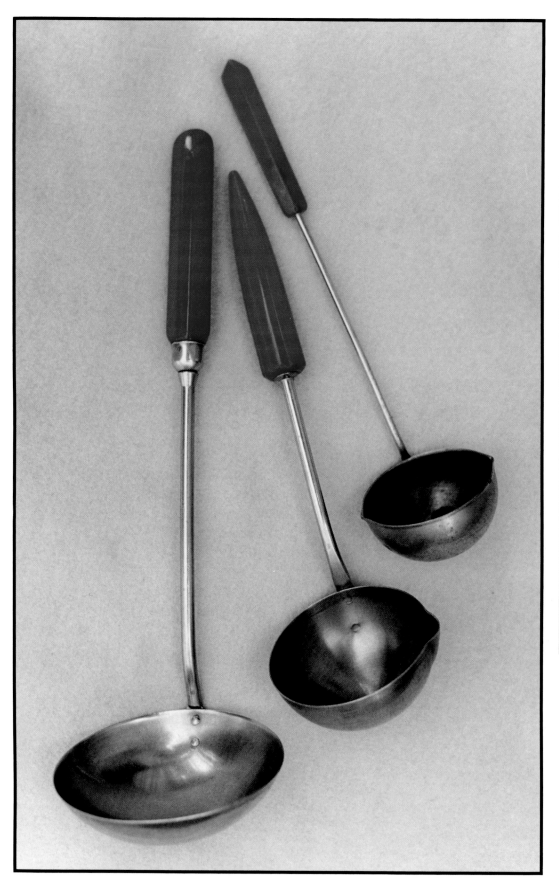

Red and yellow Androck bullet handles $35-$40 each, others $25-$30

Pastry Servers and Cheese Spreaders

Presented is a broad range of styles and prices.

Lipton Soup ran this advertisement in March 1957. $1.00 and a proof of purchase bought a four-piece set in "simulated Brazilian horn handles" which included a pastry server and cheese spreader. Today this is about the least favorite color for a Bakelite handle among collectors.

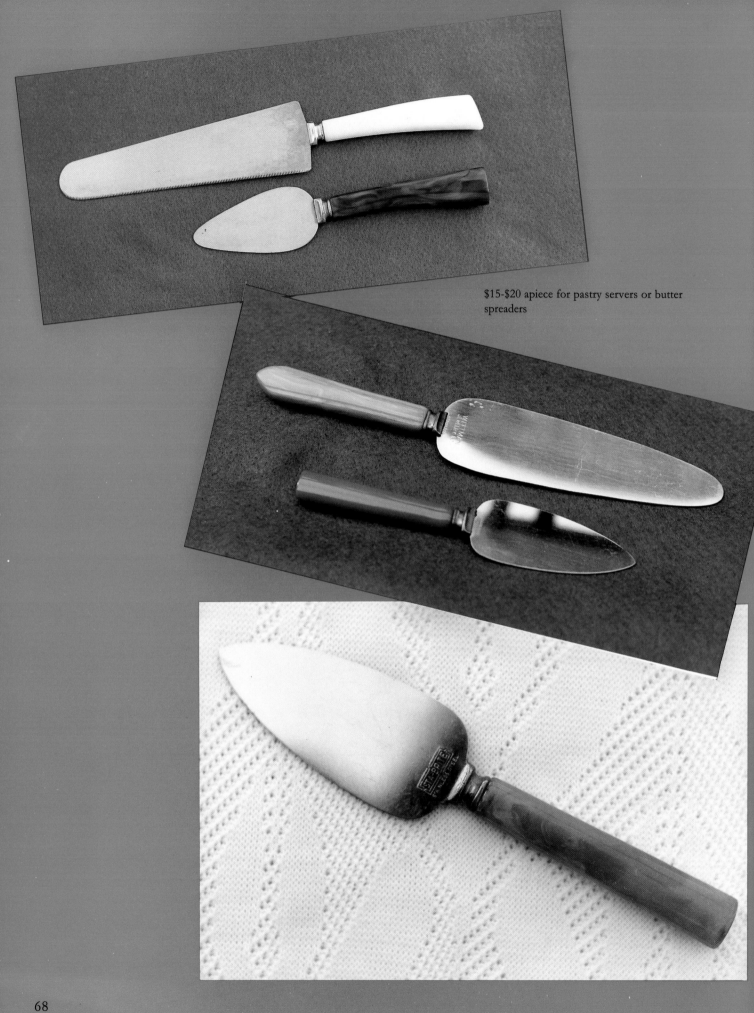

$15-$20 apiece for pastry servers or butter spreaders

Two-toned handles are difficult to find and
highly desired. $75-$100 apiece

69

$20-$25 each

Wild and wonderful, these pastry servers are a rare find! $100-$125 each

An advertisement in *Ladies' Home Journal* from February 1952 utilized a red Bakelite-handled pastry server.

The *America Home*, March 1941, pictured a green Bakelite-handled pastry server in this advertisement for Gold Medal Flour.

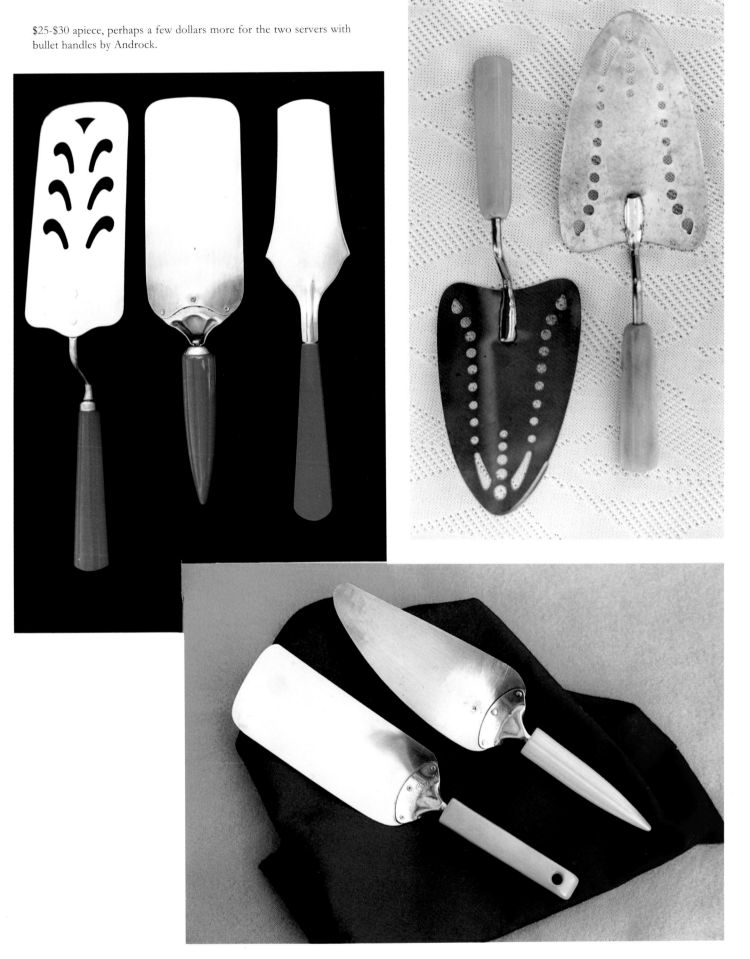

$25-$30 apiece, perhaps a few dollars more for the two servers with bullet handles by Androck.

Pizza Cutters

Pizza cutters are not frequently seen, and this is the only one I found. Perhaps the popularity of pizza was increasing while the use of Bakelite handles was waning.

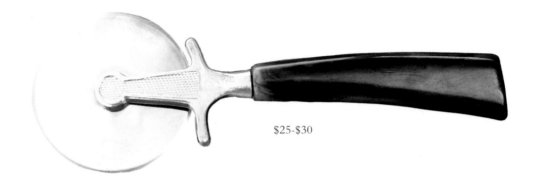

$25-$30

Serving Spoons

More than a dozen serving spoons are shown in this section. Except for bullet handles or measuring gradations, most serving spoons are worth about the same amount of money. Collectors fortunate enough to find two-colored handles should be prepared to pay significantly more. Additional spoons can be found in the section "Setting the Table."

A variety of spoon styles all share the same Bakelite handle. $25-$30

This measuring spoon provides increments for 1 and 2 tablespoons and 1 and 2 teaspoons. Its uniqueness increases its value. $30-$35

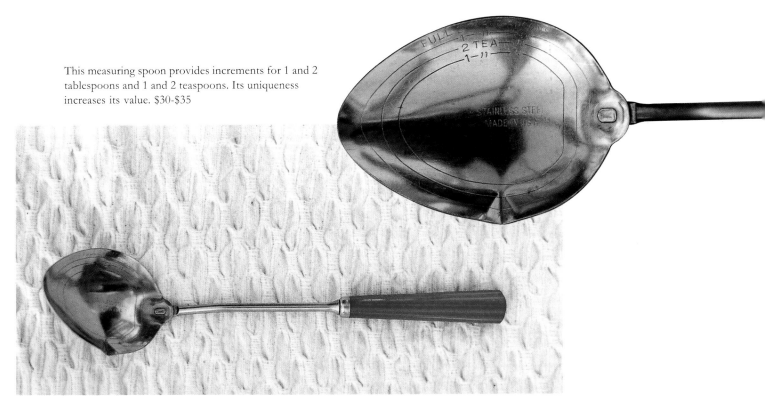

This 9" PERMA-BRITE spoon is wonderful for serving sliced tomatoes. $40-$45.

Androck made both of these stainless steel spoons. Other than the handle treatment they are identical. $25-$30 for the square-shaped handle, $30-$35 for the bullet-shaped handle

Both Androck spoons have a bullet handle. $30-$35 for either one

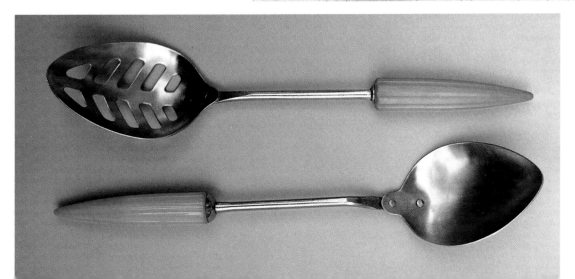

$25-$30 apiece, except for Brazilian Horn on right, $10-$12

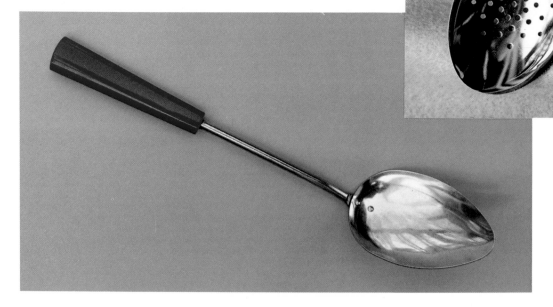

CHAPTER 3: SETTING THE TABLE

Boxed Sets and Place Settings

Customers are constantly asking me, "Where are the spoons?" Many, if not most, Bakelite sets never had spoons. As shown in these two advertisements, boxed sets usually had six forks and six knives. They were meant to be luncheon or picnic sets. Of particular interest are the two advertisements for Community Plate dating 1929 and 1930. Here the fashionable table had "jewel-like colors" and "colors blooming even on the knives." So, there was even a period of time when knives were marketed without forks. Place these knife advertisements in history and they may cause one to ponder. Six knives cost $14.00 in May of 1929. After the Great Depression began, six knives were advertised in April 1930 at a reduced cost of $9.75. The 1930 advertisement also offered the customer an opportunity to purchase a book, *Table Ways of Today* for 25 cents. In this book the use of Bakelite knives at the breakfast table is exalted. "The nicest and newest services of SILVERWARE for breakfast, for instance, burst into color in their knife-handles…that may be blue as your grapes or red as your deepest zinnias, or green as a leaf in May!"[1] The fact that households may have been suffering due to the Great Depression was not overlooked. "A woman's shelves and cupboards are her palette-her table her canvas-and her linen and china and silver and glass are her paints. And that is true, not only for breakfast, but three, four, five times a day…the newest trend of all, in the households of thousands of women-the trend that makes beauty independent of income!"[2]

Today's customers are often looking for spoons. One must be prepared to pay considerably more for Bakelite sets that include spoons, especially both teaspoons and tablespoons. Add to this the desire to have a service for twelve rather than six and the price escalates. Even when buying Bakelite pieces individually, spoons will cost more than knives and forks because there are just less of them around!

This section of the book provides a look at a variety of Bakelite sets produced to enhance the tables of the 1930s and 1940s. Various handle styles, colors, and even packaging were used. Additional forks, knives, and spoons are presented in "Handles! Handles! Handles!" just ahead.

Valley Forge Stainless Steel Made in U.S.A. $80-$95

Valley Forge Stainless Steel Made in
U.S.A. $80-$95

The *Ladies' Home Journal* from December
1939 pictures either the knife from this set
or one quite similar.

STA-BRITE Stainless Steel Made in
U.S.A. $80-$95

HULL Stainless Steel $75-$90

Landers Stainless Steel $75-$90

Universal Stainless Steel Made in U.S.A. $75-$90

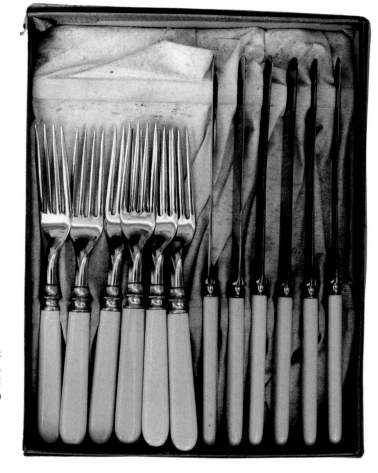

UNIVERSAL Landers, Frary &
Clark New Britain, Conn. U.S.A.
Number V73104 RESISTAIN
$75-$90

Unmarked $75-$90

82

STA-BRITE Stainless Steel Made in U.S.A. $80-$95

SHARPCUTTER Stainless Steel $90-$110

UNIVERSAL RESISTAIN
Stainless Steel Made in
U.S.A. $80-$95

Stainless Steel $90-$110

84

UNIVERSAL Landers, Frary & Clark
New Britain, Conn. U.S.A. Number
V18920 MIRROR FINISH
RESISTAIN $80-$95

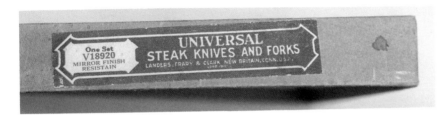

STA-BRITE Stainless Steel New Haven,
Conn. No. 25 $75-$90

Lucite, not Bakelite G.S.C.CO.
Stainless Steel $80-$95

This set came in a wooden box that opens
from the center to both the left and the right.

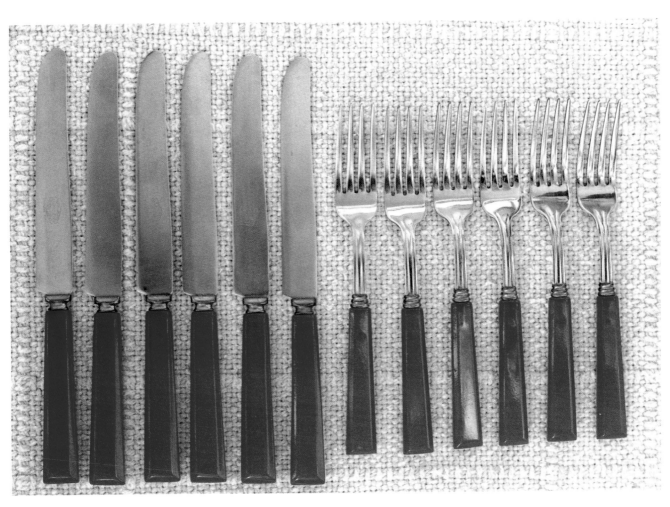

ROYAL BRAND CUTLERY COMPANY Stainless Steel $8-$10 per utensil

Stored inside is a service for twelve. Valley Forge Stainless Steel Made in U.S.A. $125-$150

Shur Edged Stainless Steel service for six, complete with a
butter knife and sugar spoon $200-$250

Englishtown Stainless Steel
service for eight in Bakelite and
Lucite $750-$800

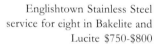

STA-BRITE Stainless Steel U.S.A. complete service for six
including a butter knife and sugar spoon $400-$450

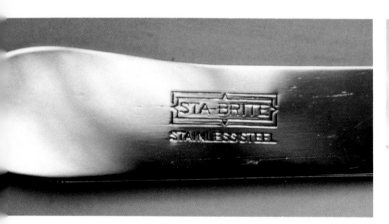

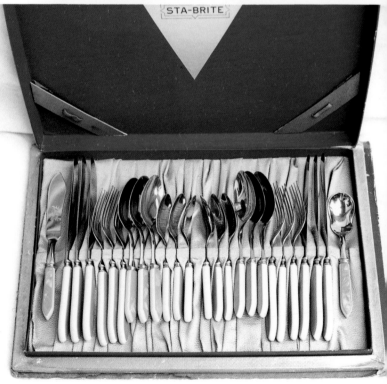

Stainless Steel $8-$10 per utensil

MOLLY PITCHER QUALITY CUTLERY
Steel Made in U.S.A. service for six in two-
toned Bakelite- red with a butterscotch
diagonal $1000

STA-BRITE ALLEGHENY Stainless Steel
Made in U.S.A. $8-$10 per utensil

Forks: Chrome Stainless Plate $6-$8 each, Table
knives: Stainless Steel $8-$10 each,
Sharp knife: $8-$10

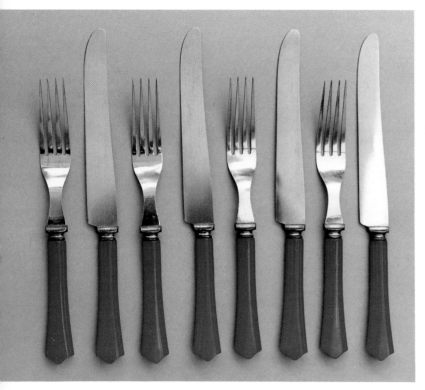

Stainless Steel $8-$10 per utensil

General Stainless Steel $8-$10 per utensil

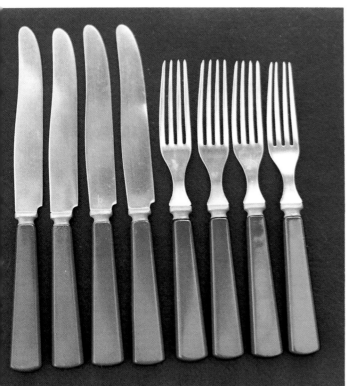

DS Stainless $8-$10 per utensil

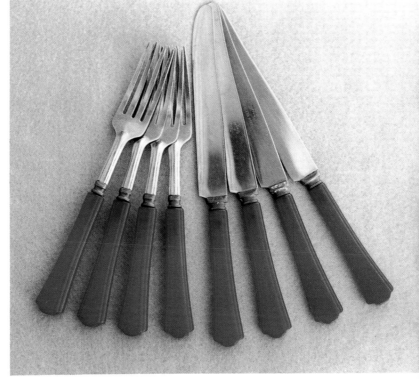

Washington Forge Stainless Steel Made in U.S.A. $8-$10 per utensil

Boker Stainless Steel Made in U.S.A. $8-$10 per utensil

Stainless Steel Made in
U.S.A. $8-$10 per utensil

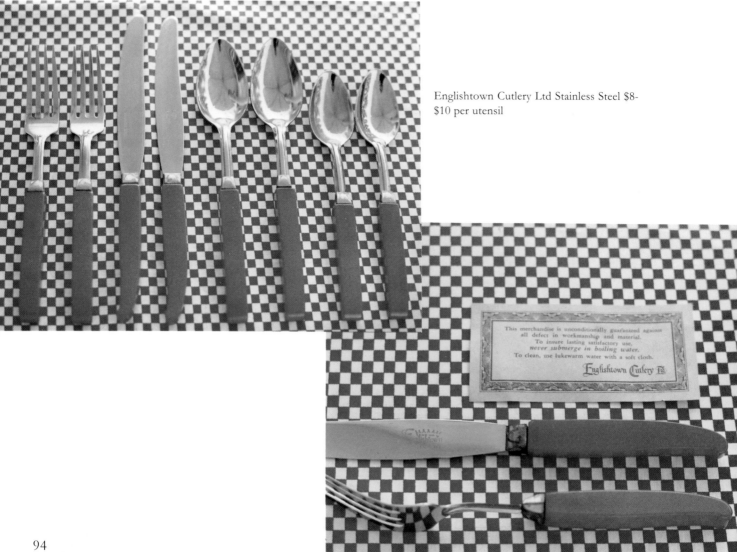

Englishtown Cutlery Ltd Stainless Steel $8-
$10 per utensil

94

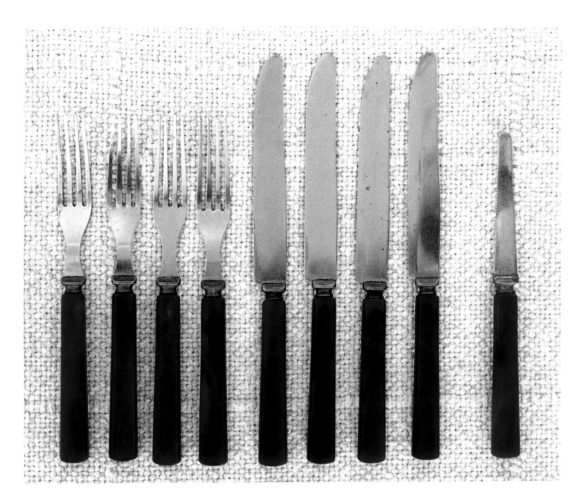

Stainless Steel $6-$8 for forks and table knives, grapefruit knife $10-$15

Robinson Knife Co. Stainless Steel $6-$8 per utensil

Forks: Chromium Stainless Plate $8-$10 each, Knives: Stainless Steel $8-$10 each

STA-BRITE Stainless Steel Made in U.S.A. $8-$10
per utensil

Forks: plated $4-$6 each, Knives: Stainless
Steel $8-$10 each

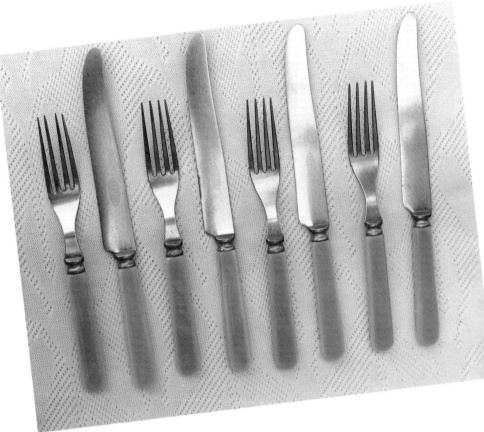

EVERBRITE Stainless Steel in cream and green $10-$12 per utensil

Stainless Steel U.S.A. $8-$10 per utensil

Englishtown Stainless Steel $8-$10 per utensil

Forks: Chromium Stainless Plate, Knives: Stainless Plate, $4-$6 per utensil

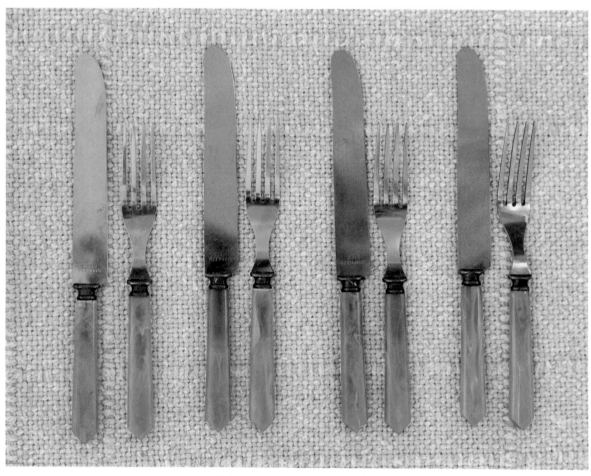

Stainless Steel $8-$10 per utensil

Boker Stainless Steel Made in U.S.A.
$8-$10 per utensil

Stainless Steel $8-$10 per utensil

Englishtown Stainless Steel fork and
knife $8-$10 each, spoons $10-$12 each

99

Washington Forge Stainless Steel Made in U.S.A. forks
and knives $8-$10 each, spoons $10-$12 each

Englishtown Cutlery Stainless Steel $25 per place
setting (fork, knife, spoon)

Stainless Steel Made in U.S.A.
$95-$110

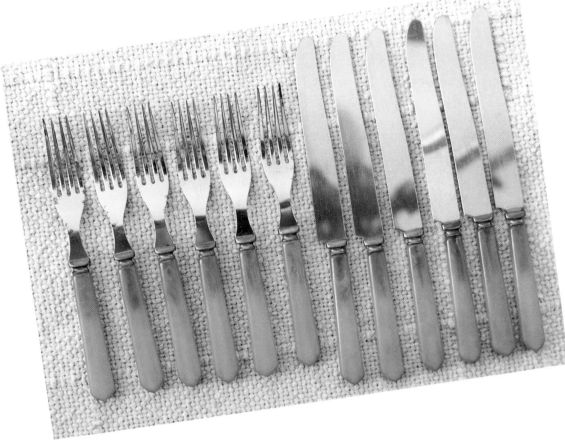

Forks: Chrome Stainless Plate $4-$6 each, Knives: Stainless Steel $6-$8 each

Royal Brand Stainless
Steel $8-$10 per utensil

Stainless Steel $8-$10 per utensil

STA-BRITE Stainless Steel Made in U.S.A $6-$8 per utensil

FIRTH STERLING Stainless Steel $8-$10 per utensil

Stainless Steel $8-$10 per utensil

Eagle Stainless Steel $6-$8 per utensil

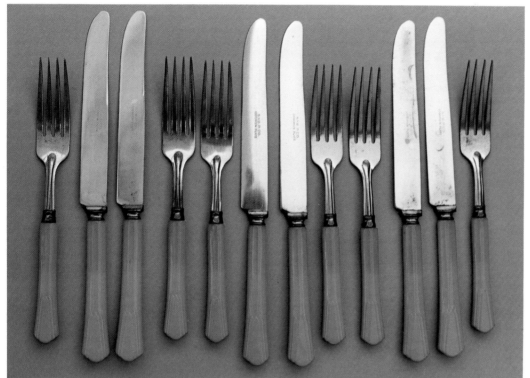

The label on the end of the box that held the forks and knives in the picture at left.

S-B.P.CO. Chromium Plate (Sta-Brite) New Haven, Conn. These utensils were produced to accompany Fiestaware and are often found in four-color sets $10-$12 per utensil

STA-BRITE Stainless Steel Made in U.S.A. This is the complete Fiesta Set shown in the original colors: cobalt blue (with age it resembles black), green, orange, and gold. No tablespoons were made for this set. $10-$12 per utensil

Detail of the Sta-Brite "Fiesta" handles

STA-BRITE ALLEGHENY Stainless Steel Made in the U.S.A. Four-color set $10-$12 per utensil

FIRTH STERLING Stainless Steel $8-$10 per utensil

VALLEY FORGE Stainless Steel $8-$10 per utensil

Stainless Steel $8-$10 per utensil

Forks: Chrome Plate, Knives: Stainless Steel
$8-$10 per utensil

Monroe Silver Co. forks, Chrome Plate; knives, Stainless Steel This incomplete set has salad/dessert forks, iced tea spoons, soup spoons, and teaspoons. $12-$15 per utensil

Stainless Steel $8-$10 per utensil

Royal Brand Cutlery Company Stainless Steel $10-$12 per utensil

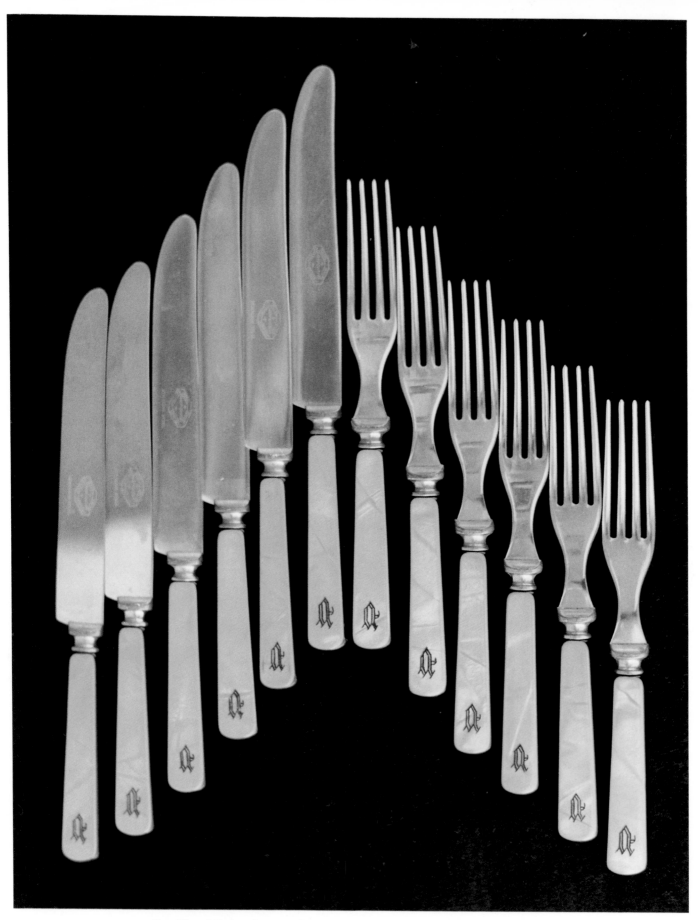

Royal Brand Cutlery Company Stainless Steel $125-$150 for the set with monograms

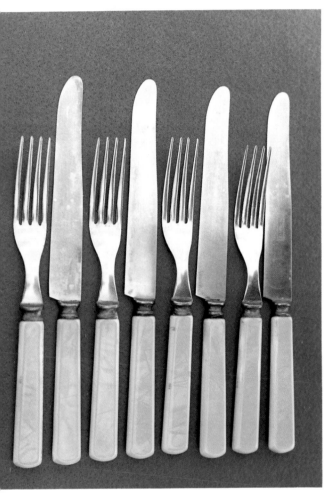

An eagle's head marks the knife blades of this pink flatware. Stainless Steel $12-$15 per utensil

STA-BRITE Stainless Steel Made in U.S.A. $10-$12 per utensil

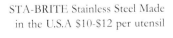
STA-BRITE Stainless Steel Made in the U.S.A $10-$12 per utensil

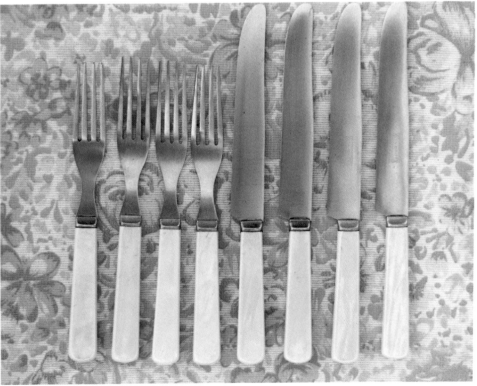

Clear Cryst Stainless Steel Bakelite and Lucite utensils $15-$20 per utensil
Not shown are green and blue with Lucite. Green $20-$24 per utensil, blue $25-$30 per utensil

Locating all five pieces for a complete place setting can be a challenge! $15-$20 per utensil

Here is a comparison of the two Clear Cryst styles in the previous pictures.

Red Lucite and Bakelite $15-$20 per utensil

Washington Forge Stainless Steel Made in the U.S.A. Red Lucite and Bakelite $15-$20 per utensil

Contrasting Bakelite spades, hearts, clubs, and diamonds are inserted into the handles of these utensils. A complete set as shown is very rare. $800-$1000

Stainless Steel $25-$30 per place setting

Englishtown Stainless Steel $25-30 per place setting

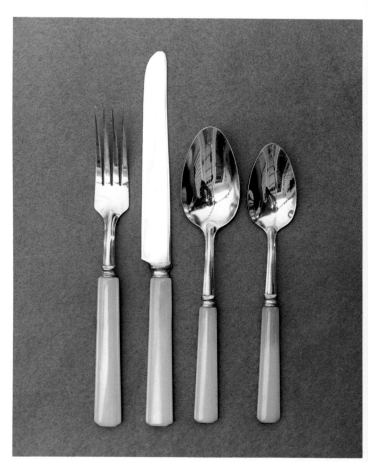

Stainless Steel Made in U.S.A.
$25-$30 per place setting

Stainless Steel $25-$30 per place setting

GENERAL CUTLERY CO.
Stainless Steel Made in U.S.A. $25-
$30 per place setting

PEERLESS Stainless Steel $25-$30 per place setting

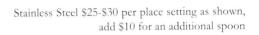

Stainless Steel $25-$30 per place setting as shown,
add $10 for an additional spoon

Left: Washington Forge
Stainless Steel Made in the
U.S.A. $8-$10 per utensil
Right: Stainless Steel $8-$10
per utensil

Federal Stainless Steel $6-$8 per utensil

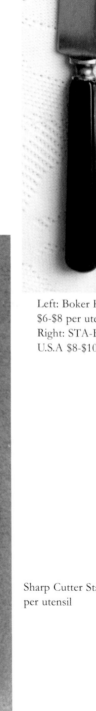

Left: Boker Hammer Forged Stainless Steel $6-$8 per utensil
Right: STA-BRITE Stainless Steel Made in U.S.A $8-$10 per utensil

Sharp Cutter Stainless Steel $6-$8 per utensil

Left to right: GSC CO Stainless Steel, Megheny Forge Stainless Steel, Federal Stainless Steel, Stainless Steel $6-$8 per utensil

Left: Stainless Steel $6-$8 per utensil
Middle: STA-BRITE Stainless Steel $4-$6 per utensil
Right: S.B. (Sta-Brite) Stainless Steel two toned green and black $10-$12 per utensil

Federal Stainless Steel (both sets) $6-$8 per utensil

Fork: Chrome Stainless
Plate, Knife: Stainless Steel
$8-$10 per utensil

Stainless Steel $8-$10 per
utensil

Fork: B.K.CO.Stainless Steel,
Knife: BESTEEL Stainless Steel
$8-$10 per utensil

STA-BRITE Stainless Steel Made in
U.S.A. $8-$10 per utensil

RARE Polkadot handles $200+ per utensil

RARE Checkerboard handles
$200+ per utensil

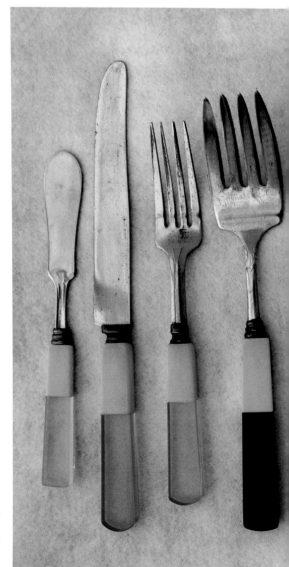

Bakelite and Lucite handle left to right: butter knife
$30-$40, knife $20-$25, fork $20-$25, serving (salad)
fork Perma-brite $40-$50

120

Tri-color Bakelite handles $100-$125 each

Bakelite and Lucite butter knives $30-$40 and teaspoons $20-$25

VOOS Stainless Steel knives and spoons in
cream and green $8-$10 per utensil

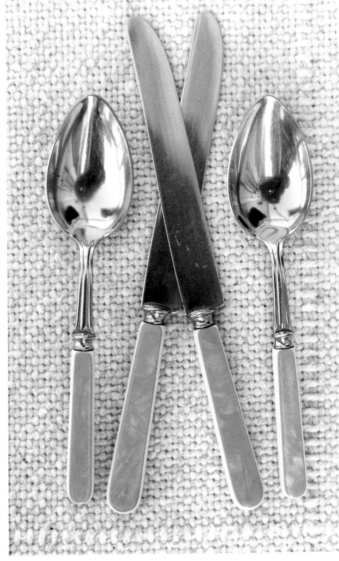

121

Corn Holders

The colors and textures of Bakelite are never more evident than when looking at something as seemingly meaningless as corn holders. These clever little spiked gadgets get pushed into the ends of a cob of corn thus providing a "civilized" manner for dining on this often messy summer treat. A display published in July 1945 in *Better Homes and Gardens* shows red Bakelite corn holders.

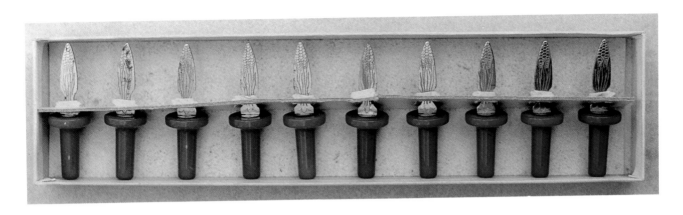

Boxed set in Kelly Green $125-$150

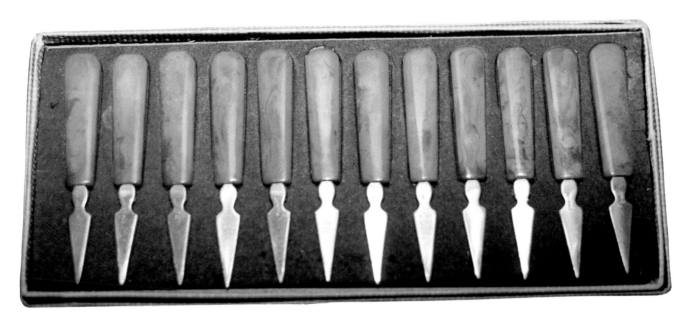

Stainless Steel $90-$110 for boxed set

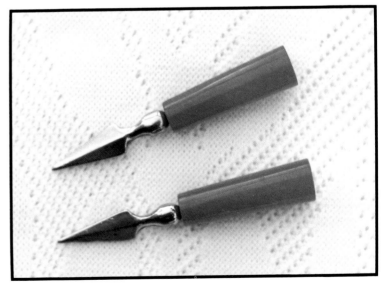

$20-$30 per pair

$15-$25 per pair

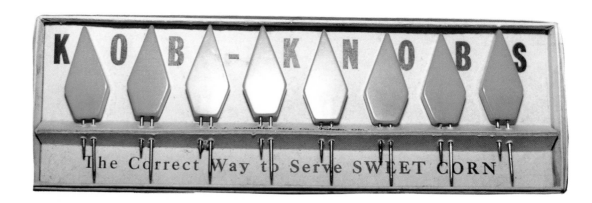

KOB-KNOBS were manufactured by C.J. Schneider Mfg. Co, Toledo, Ohio, and were also produced in Kelly Green. Although there are fewer pairs of corn holders in these boxes compared to the other boxed set, this design is a more popular one among collectors. $90-$110 for boxed set

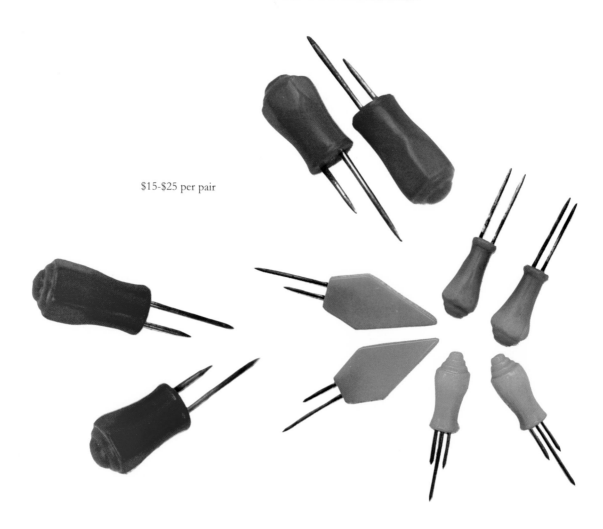

$15-$25 per pair

$15-$25 per pair

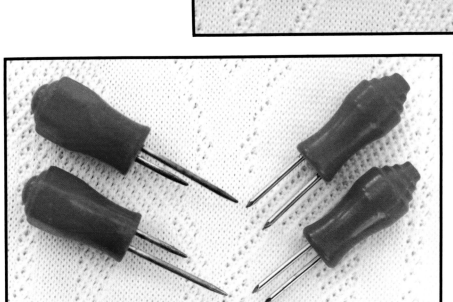

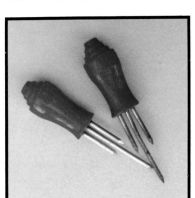

125

Handles! Handles! Handles!

The varieties and styles of Bakelite flatware seem end-less. The pieces I have documented represent a sampling of the bountiful choices available to the collector. While working on this project I located countless single pieces of Bakelite, a knife here, a fork there, each with no additional matches to create a table setting. This section offers these forks, knives, and spoons for your enjoyment.

When setting your table, anything goes! Be as eclectic and spontaneous as you choose. Even in June 1940, *The American Home* magazine set a table using Bakelite in multiple colors and handle designs.

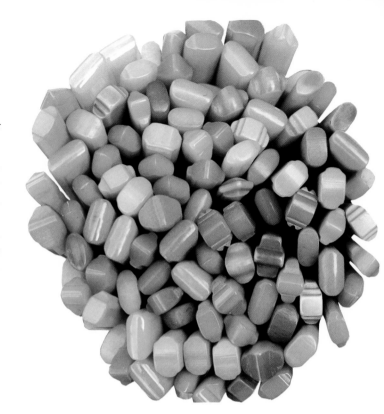

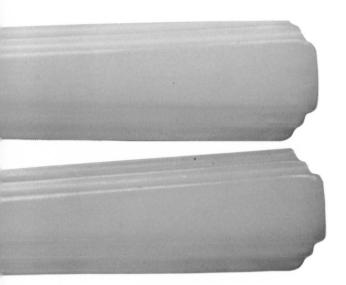

This illustrates the minute differences between some handles. The pair of handles on the left are similar to but not an exact match with the pair on the right.

Forks

Six matched Stainless Steel
forks $8-$10 each

Six matched Stainless Steel forks $8-$10 each

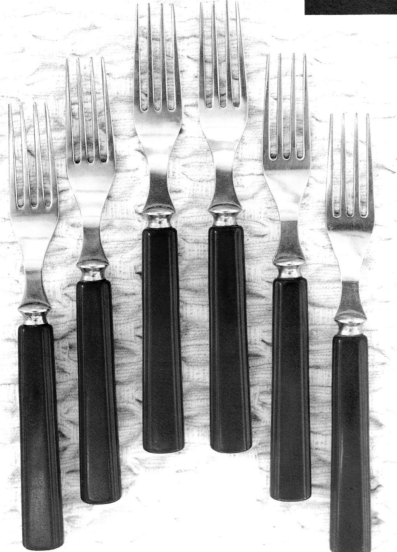

Four different handles $8-$10 each

Six matched forks $8-$10 each

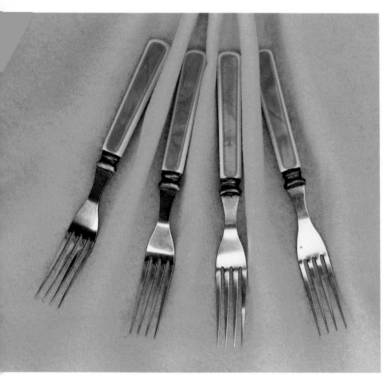

Four matching cream and green Stainless Steel forks $8-$10 each

Seven different handles $8-$10 each

This Stainless Steel fork is an unusual size. The overall length is slightly longer than 8 inches, and the Bakelite handle is 4.5 inches. $8-$10

Four different handles $8-$10 each

Five matching Stainless Steel forks made in the U.S.A. $8-$10 each

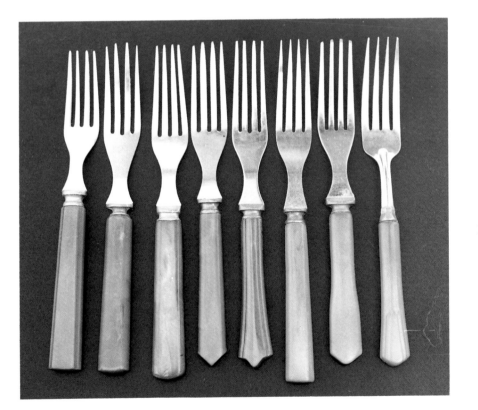

Eight different handles $8-$10 each

129

Seven matching Stainless Steel forks $8-$10 each

Tri-color Bakelite fork $50-$60, chevron $100-$125

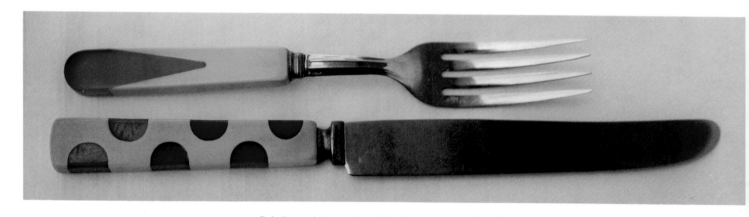

Bakelite and Lucite fork $35-$50, polkadot knife $200+

Knives

Six different handles $8-$10 each

Six different handles $8-$10 each

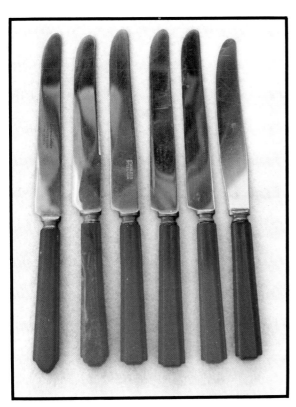

Six different handles $8-$10 each

Six different handles $8-$10 each

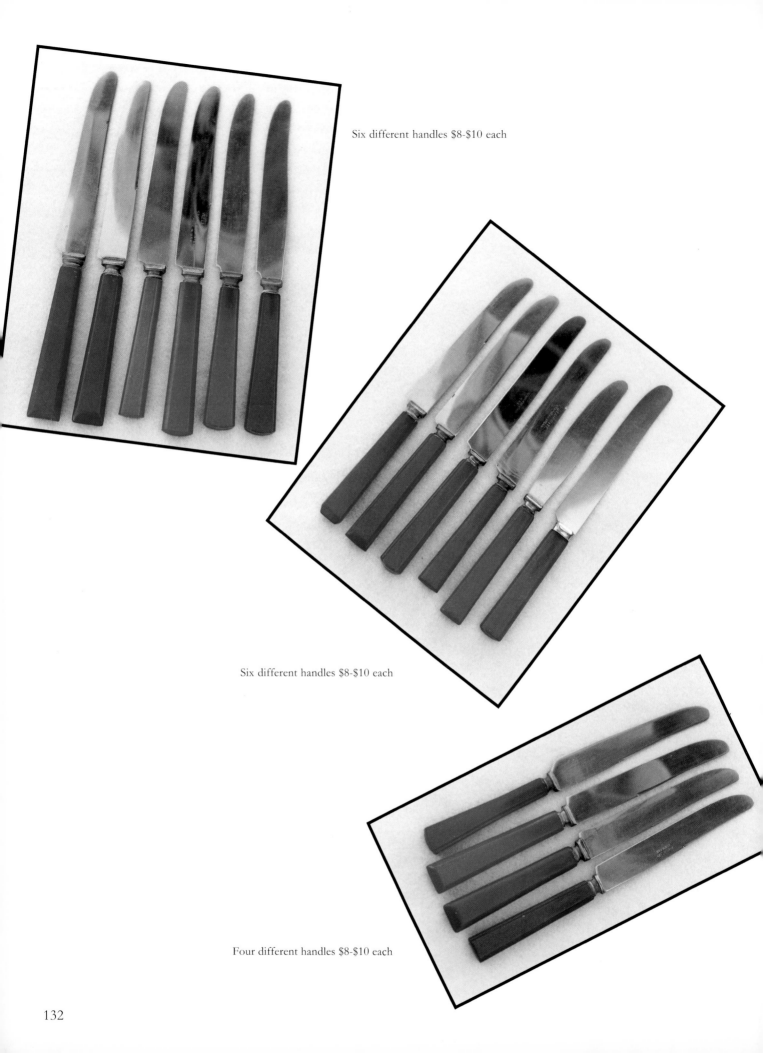

Six different handles $8-$10 each

Six different handles $8-$10 each

Four different handles $8-$10 each

Eight different handles $8-$10 each

Eight different handles $8-$10 each

Seven different handles $8-$10 each

Seven different handles $8-$10 each

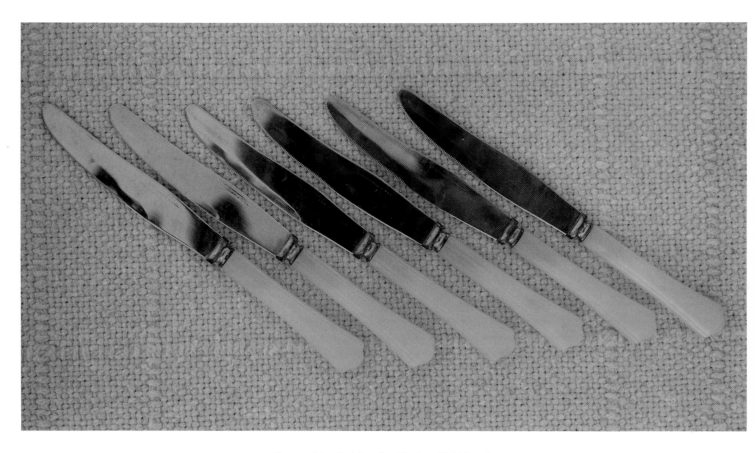

Six matching Stainless Steel knives $8-$10 each

Six different handles $8-$10 each

Six different handles $8-$10 each

Six different handles $8-$10 each

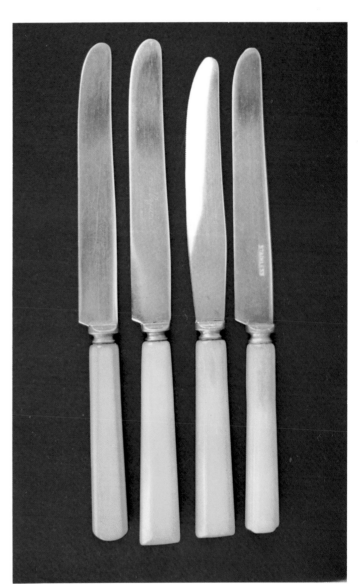

Four different handles $8-$10 each

Six different handles $8-$10 each

Six different handles $8-$10 each

Six different handles $8-$10 each

Six different handles $8-$10 each

136

Six different handles $8-$10 each

Five different handles $8-$10 each

Although these knives may appear to be part of a multi-colored set, they in fact do not match. The knife with a black Bakelite handle is marked "Made in U.S.A." The yellow knife is unmarked and has a beveled edge at the top of the knife blade. $8-$10 each

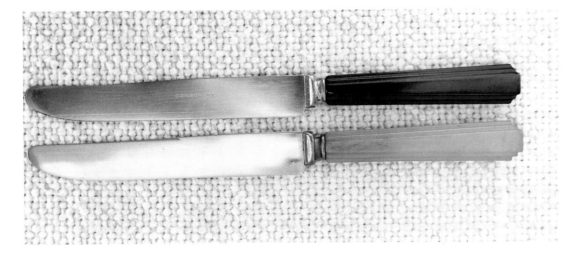

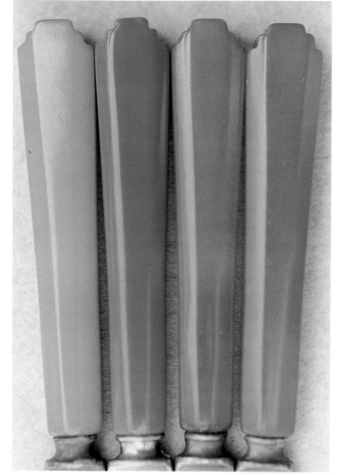

Three different handles $8-$10 each

Hampshire made a four-color set in gold, periwinkle, green, and orange. Here is a close-up of the manufacturer's marking on a knife blade. The green and gold knives would cost $6-8 each if found separately. The orange knife would be slightly more at $10-$12. The periwinkle would be a real find at any price! ($20-$25) Remember, too, the set is worth more than the individual pieces.

Three different handles $8-$10 each

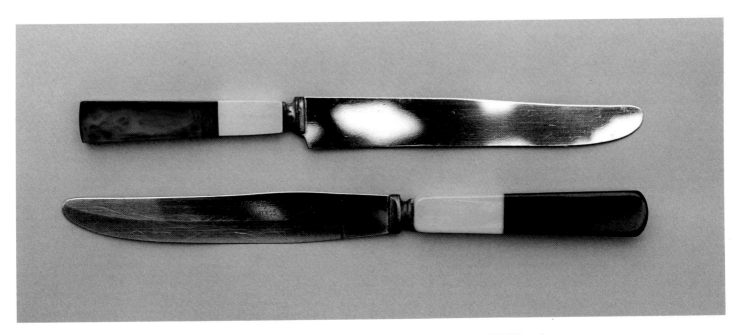

Washington Forge Stainless Steel, Bakelite and Lucite $20-$25 each

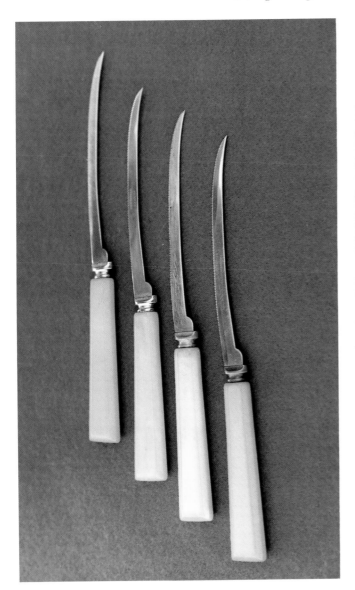

Four matching Henry's Stainless Tomato and Steak
Knives $8-$10 each

Three different tomato/steak knives red-$15-$18 each, brown-$8-$10

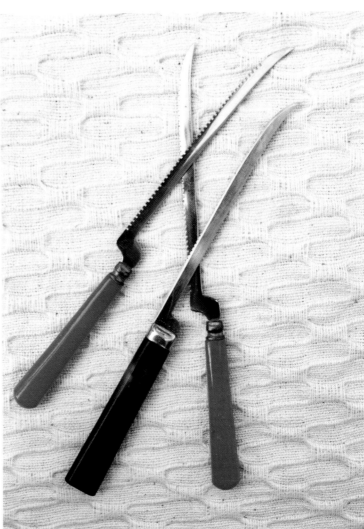

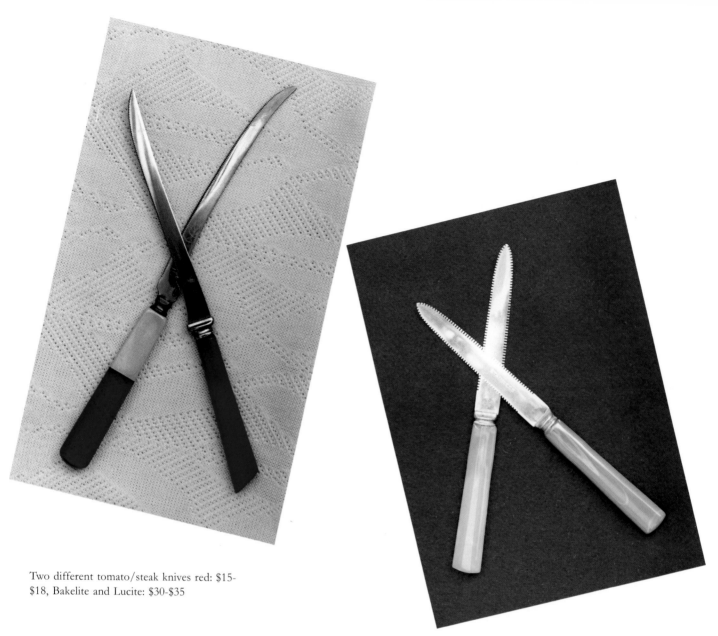

Two different tomato/steak knives red: $15-$18, Bakelite and Lucite: $30-$35

Two different Stainless Steel grapefruit knives $10-$15 each

Henry's Original Tomato & Steak Knife (Henry Fox sole distributor, 3203 Atlantic Avenue) in cream and green $22-$25; Stainless Steel grapefruit knife in cream and green $22-$25

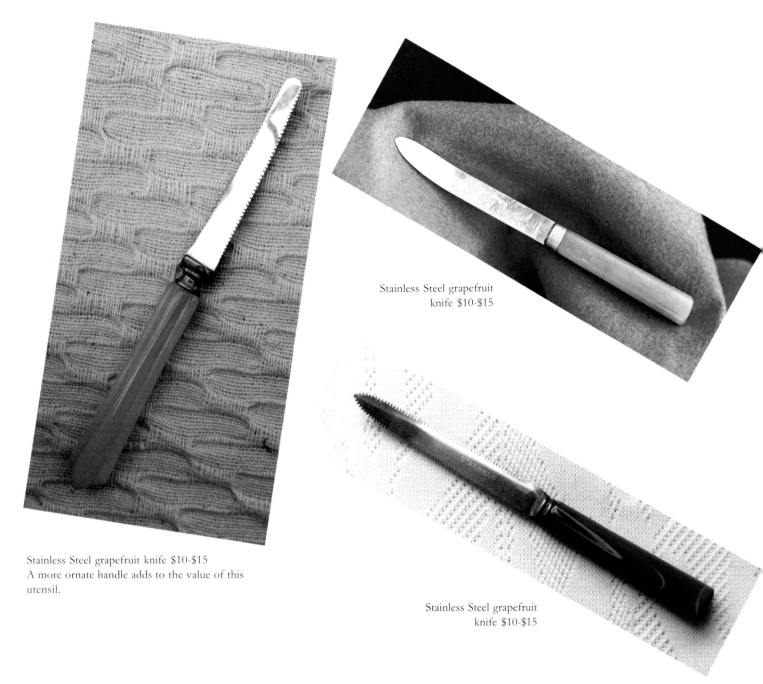

Stainless Steel grapefruit
knife $10-$15

Stainless Steel grapefruit knife $10-$15
A more ornate handle adds to the value of this
utensil.

Stainless Steel grapefruit
knife $10-$15

Grapefruit knife: Federal
Stainless Steel Made in
U.S.A. $20-$22, Paring
knife: STA-BRITE Stainless
Steel Made in U.S.A. $8-$10

Grapefruit knife: $10-$15,
Paring knives $8-$10

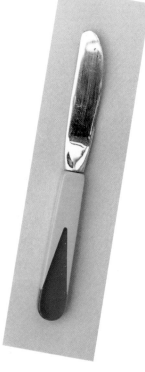

Bakelite and Lucite 6-inch knife
in Stainless Steel $35-$50

Boxed set of "Dinkee" Knives each measuring 4.5 inches. This set was issued in
1967 to commemorate the Canadian Centennial. $45-$60 for the set

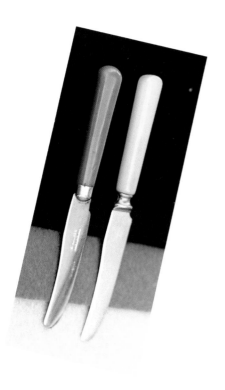

Two fruit knives similar to the "Dinkee" Knives
Yellow: Stainless Steel $8-$10, Green: Stainless
Steel Made in England $8-$10

Six matching ROSTFREI SOLINGEN 6.5-inch Bakelite and Lucite
fruit knives $175-$200 for the set

Valley Forge Stainless Steel Made
in U.S.A. $8-$10

Four matching Stainless Steel fruit/cheese knives Made in U.S.A. $35-$45 for the set

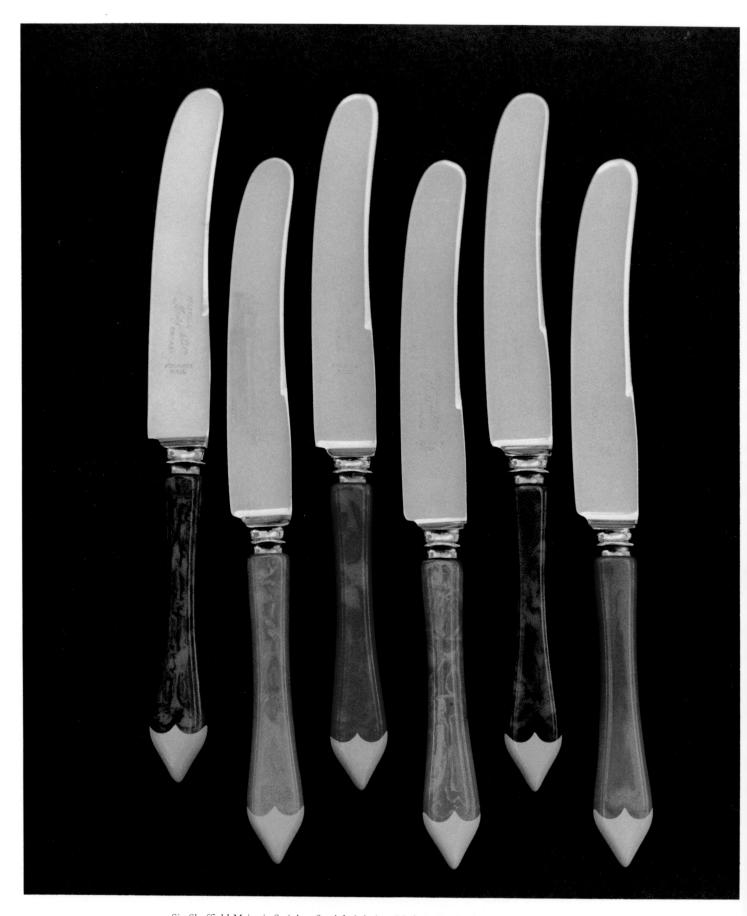

Six Sheffield Majestic Stainless Steel fruit knives Made in England $175-$200 for the set

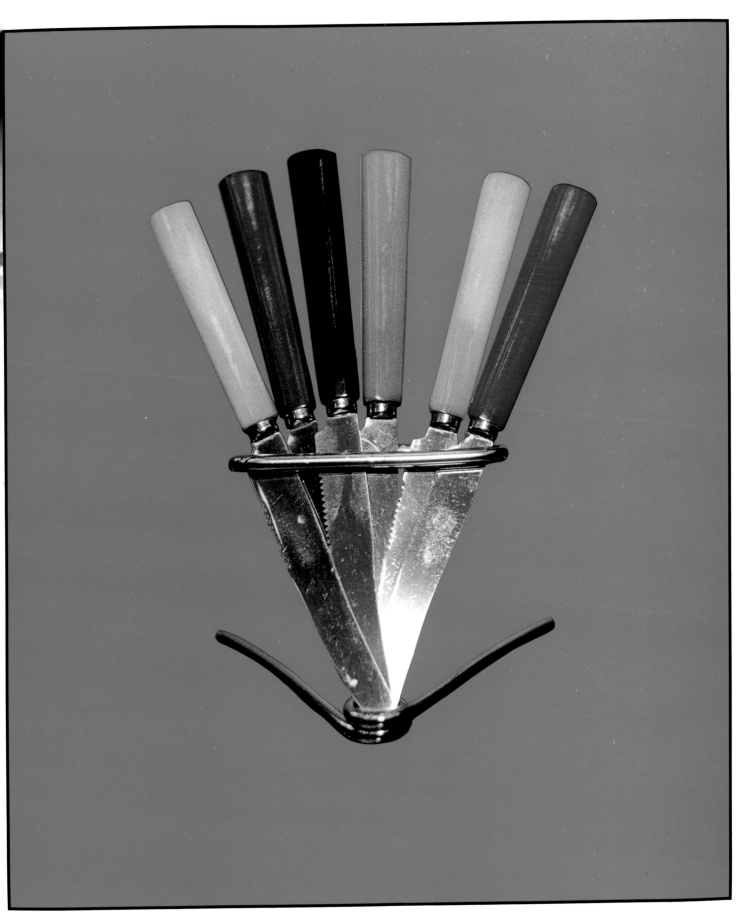

Six ROSTFREI SOLINGEN fruit knives in a metal stand $150-$175 for the set

Four matching Englishtown Cutlery Ltd. Stainless Steel knives Made in Sheffield, England $35-$45 for the set

Four matching Stainless Steel knives $35-$45 for the set

Four matching Stainless Steel knives Made in U.S.A. $30-$35 for the set

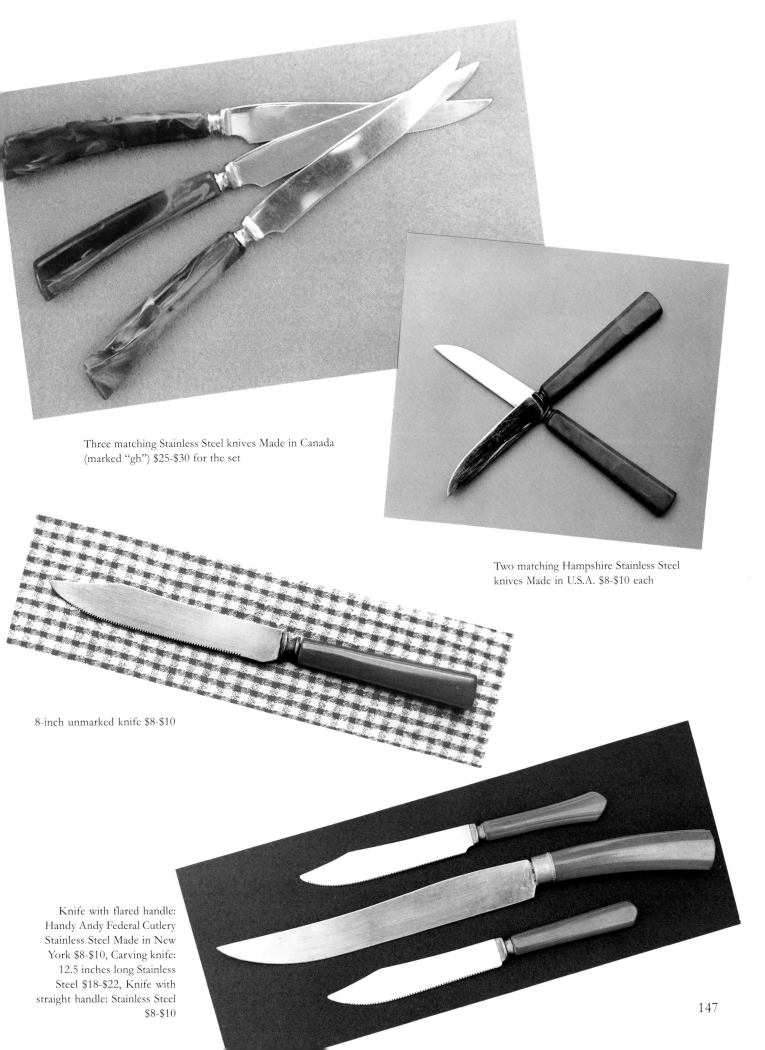

Three matching Stainless Steel knives Made in Canada (marked "gh") $25-$30 for the set

Two matching Hampshire Stainless Steel knives Made in U.S.A. $8-$10 each

8-inch unmarked knife $8-$10

Knife with flared handle: Handy Andy Federal Cutlery Stainless Steel Made in New York $8-$10, Carving knife: 12.5 inches long Stainless Steel $18-$22, Knife with straight handle: Stainless Steel $8-$10

Green: The Burns Slice" Stainless Steel
Made in Canada $18-$22
Red: Robinson Knife Co. Stainless Steel
Made in U.S.A $18-$22
Yellow: Burns Mfg. Co. Serrated
Stainless Steel Made in Syracuse, New
York, $8-$10

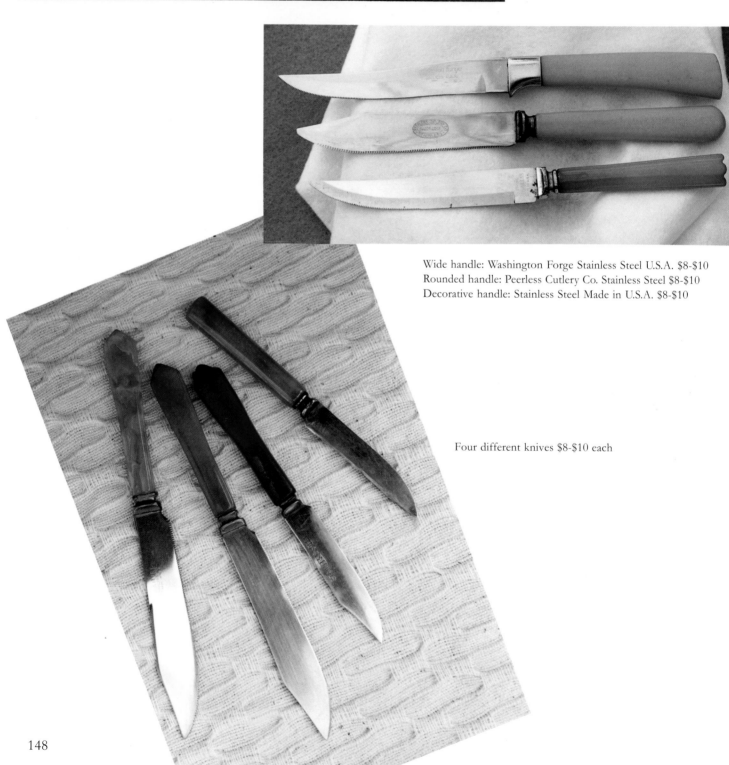

Wide handle: Washington Forge Stainless Steel U.S.A. $8-$10
Rounded handle: Peerless Cutlery Co. Stainless Steel $8-$10
Decorative handle: Stainless Steel Made in U.S.A. $8-$10

Four different knives $8-$10 each

Four different knives all about 12 inches long
$18-$22 apiece

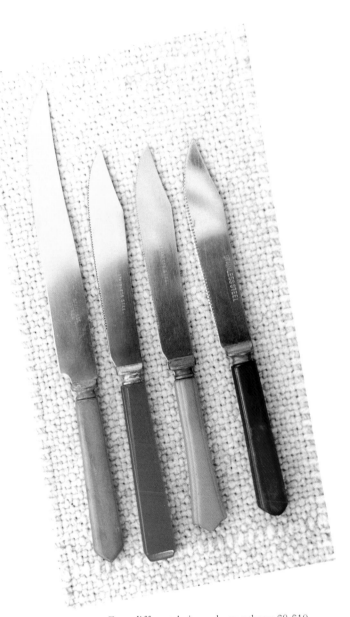

Four different knives, shorter three: $8-$10,
longer one: $12-$15

Straight handle with blunt end: STA-BRITE Stainless Steel Made in U.S.A $8-$10
Wider handle with pointed end: Handy Andy Federal Cutlery Co. Stainless Steel $8-$10

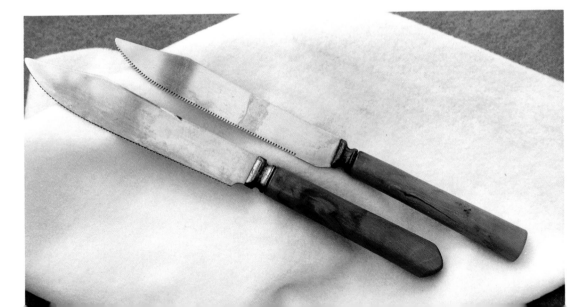

Four different knives $8-$10 each

Four different knives, shorter three are 8.5-9.75
inches in length $12-$15 apiece, longer one, Cayuga
Stainless Steel 12 inches long $18-$22

Three different knives
$8-$10 each

Two different knives
$8-$10 each

Three knives, two that match: acadia Stainless
Steel Made in Canada $12-$15 each

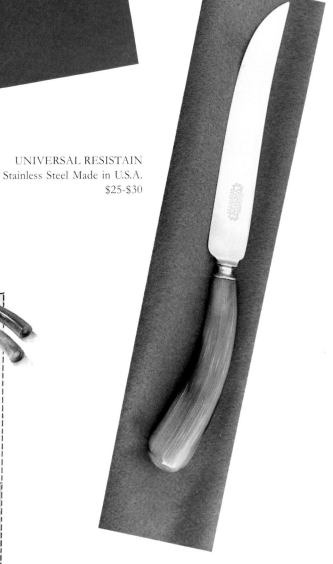

UNIVERSAL RESISTAIN
Stainless Steel Made in U.S.A.
$25-$30

The November 1950 issue of *The American Home*
shows a carving set very similar to the Universal
carving knife.

151

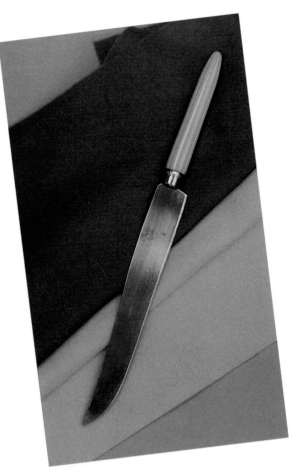

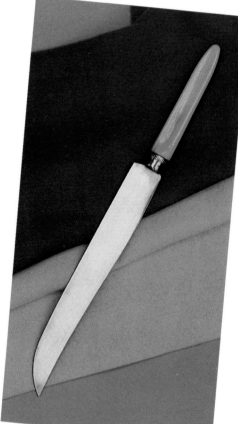

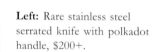

These pictures show both sides of the "semi-bullet" handle on this carving knife. Additional pieces with this handle are pictured in "Carving Sets and Meat Forks."

$8-$10

Six different carving knives $18-$22 apiece

Left: Rare stainless steel serrated knife with polkadot handle, $200+.

Right: This 8" knife/letter opener is popular as a Bakelite collectible and as World's Fair memorabilia. The blade is marked, "Chicago World's Fair 1934." $50-$60.

Two different knives $12-15 apiece

Three different knives $12-$15 each

Four different knives $8-$10 each

Three different knives $8-$10 each

153

Three different knives $8-$10 each

Two different knives $8-$10 each

Justinus Stainless Steel Solingen,
Germany, $20-$25

Green: MARVEL Stainless Steel Made in U.S.A. $8-$10
Red: HANDY ANDY Federal Cutlery Co. Stainless Steel
Made in U.S.A. $8-$10
Yellow: Stainless Steel $8-$10

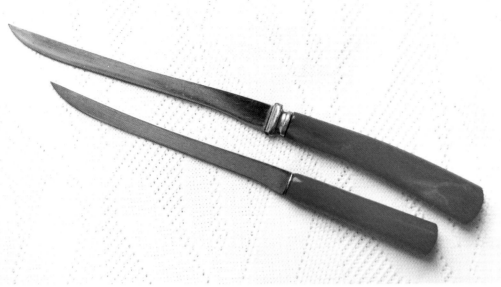

Two red knives $15-$18

Straight handle: bar tool/knife forged Stainless
REGENT Sheffield, England 8.5 inches $20-$25
Curved handle: NICHT ROSTEND GRANTON
D.R.PAT. 509838 $10-$12

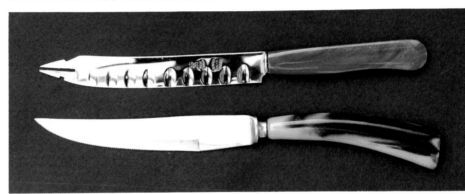

Two Bakelite and Lucite knives, 7.25 and 6 inches $35-$50 apiece

Orange: rare color! Stainless Steel DES-PAT
96,720 11.75 inches long $30-$35
Yellow and black: ROBINSON KNIFE CO.
Stainless Steel 12.25 inches long $25-$40

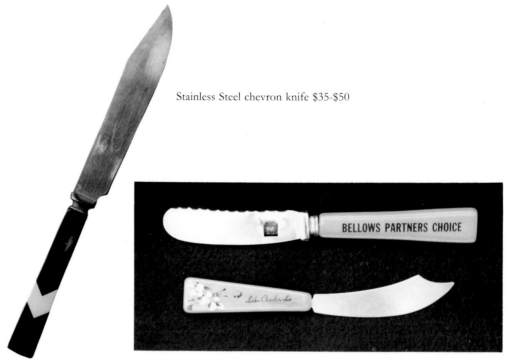

Stainless Steel chevron knife $35-$50

Two advertising knives $20-$25

Two chevron knives $35-$50 each

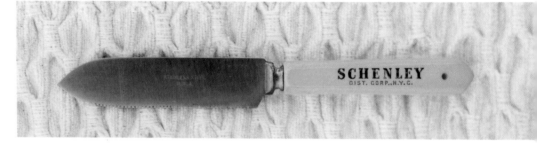

Advertising knife $15-$18

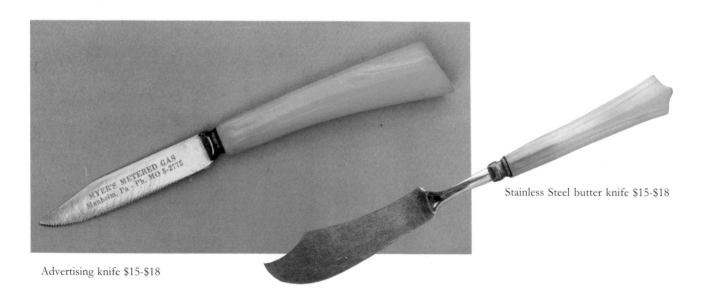

Advertising knife $15-$18

Stainless Steel butter knife $15-$18

Three utensils with inset Bakelite silhouettes RARE! $150-$175 apiece

World's Fair knife RARE! $175-$200

Orange butter knife $18-$20

Yellow butter knife: PERMA-BRITE $15-$18
Cobalt blue butter knife: UNIVERSAL $15-$18

Stainless Steel butter
knife $15-$18

Butter knife and sugar spoon $15-$18 each

Red and yellow butter knives: S-B (Sta-
Brite) Stainless Steel Made in U.S.A.
$15-$18 apiece
Gold butter knife with ornate handle:
Stainless Steel $18-$20

Spoons

The price of any teaspoon or tablespoon will always exceed that of its matching fork or knife. When part of a set, or with a complete table setting, the price increases even further. The scarcity of and demand for spoons simply makes them cost more.

Fruit cocktail is being served with a Bakelite spoon in this March 1949 advertisement found in *The American Home.*

Van Camp's Pork and Beans drip from a red Bakelite-handled spoon in this *Ladies' Home Journal* advertisement from August 1952.

The Holiday House offered a "Spoon Drip" for sale in 1950. Shown with the merchandise are three Bakelite-handled spoons.

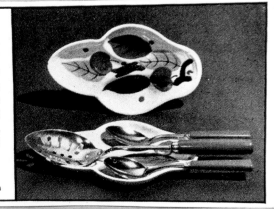

HOME ON THE RANGE
Hand painted cherry design China "Spoon Drip." Holds three spoons; hole at top for hanging when not in use. Keeps stove top free from mess and utensil stains. Has gay verse tag. Price (no COD's) $1.95 ppd.

THE HOLIDAY HOUSE
P. O. Box 554, Oshkosh, Wisconsin

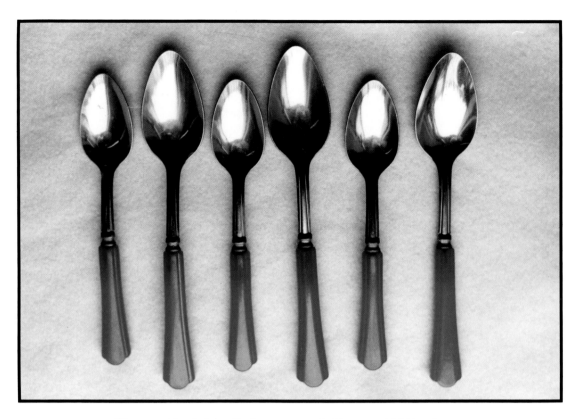

Three matching Stainless Steel teaspoons and tablespoons $8-$10 each

Six EKCO Stainless Steel spoons Made in U.S.A. $8-$10 each

Four matching S.B. (Sta-Brite) Stainless Steel teaspoons and tablespoons $6-8 each due to the white plastic connecting the metal to the Bakelite.

Hampshire Stainless Steel available in four colors
Two matching teaspoons and tablespoons $8-$10 each

Six matching Stainless Steel tablespoons Made in U.S.A. $6-$8 each due to the white plastic connecting the metal to the Bakelite

Six matching teaspoons with unusually pointy bowls $8-$10 each

Four matching Stainless Steel teaspoons Made in U.S.A. $6-$8 each due to the white plastic connecting the metal to the Bakelite

Two groupings of matching table-spoons Stainless Steel Made in U.S.A. plastic connectors-$6-$8 each, metal connectors $8-$10 each

Four matching teaspoons and three matching tablespoons N.S.CO. Stainless Steel $8-$10 each

Three matching tablespoons and two matching teaspoons OS Made in U.S.A. $8-$10 each

Two matching tablespoons and one matching teaspoon $8-$10 each

Six matching tablespoons $10-$12 each

Two sets of matching tablespoons all Bakelite, $8-$10 each; Bakelite and Lucite, $20-$25 each

Stainless Steel tablespoon $8-$10 each

Two pairs of matching Stainless Steel tablespoons $8-$10 each

Three different Stainless Steel teaspoons
$8-$10 each

Four different spoons, plastic connector,
$6-$8; others $8-$10 each

Six different Stainless Steel tablespoons $8-$10 each

Three different Stainless Steel
tablespoons $8-$10 each

Three different Stainless Steel spoons $8-$10 each

Six different Stainless Steel spoons $8-$10 each

Stainless Steel teaspoon $8-$10 each

Four different spoons $8-$10 each

D&S soup spoon $10-$12

Stainless Steel chevron
spoon $35-$50

Six Stainless Steel spoons with the same Bakelite handle design $8-$10 each

S-B (Sta-Brite) Stainless Steel Made in U.S.A.
sugar spoon with plastic connector $12-$15

167

Matching sugar spoon and butter knife S.B. (Sta-Brite) Stainless Steel Made in U.S.A. $12-$15 each

Three iced tea spoons almost 10 inches long $15-$18 each

Red sugar spoon: S-B (Sta-Brite) Stainless Steel U.S.A with plastic connector $12-$15
Brown sugar spoon: N.S.O. PERMA-BRITE $15-$18

Iced teaspoon almost 12 inches long Stainless Steel Made in U.S.A $18-$20

Iced teaspoon 9.5 inches long $15-$18

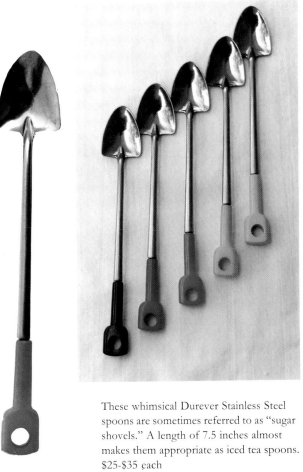

These whimsical Durever Stainless Steel spoons are sometimes referred to as "sugar shovels." A length of 7.5 inches almost makes them appropriate as iced tea spoons. $25-$35 each

DS iced tea spoon 7.5 inches long $15-$18

Matching Stainless Steel iced tea spoons $15-$18 each

Six matching iced tea spoons $25-$35 each

Twelve N.S.CO Chrome iced tea spoons, three black (cobalt?), gold, orange, and green $25-$35 each

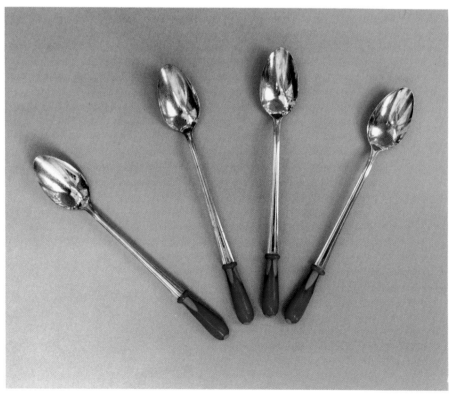

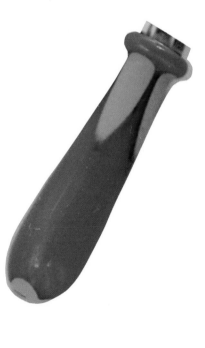

Four N.S.CO. Chrome red-orange and gold iced tea spoons $25-$35 each

Napkin Rings

Napkin rings are jewelry for the table, and as with any fine gemstones finding them can be as challenging as affording them. But what an intrinsic reward for collectors who have success locating these colorful, fanciful delights!

The pieces shown here come from a single collection! One can only imagine the time, energy, and fun in putting together such a phenomenal display. Assessing value becomes difficult because there are pieces here I have never seen before. For an enthusiastic, motivated collector to discover an item that is new to him or her, how much would that person pay to possess such a treasure? I am placing a range of value that must be interpreted as a guide and not prices "carved in stone." To see a needed piece for the first time, an advanced collector may be willing to pay a lot of money to acquire it.

A point of interest in the value of figural napkin rings: generally napkin rings that have eyes made from a contrasting Bakelite color have a greater value than those with painted on eyes or no eyes at all.

The sitting dogs have painted eyes and the standing dogs have "rodded" eyes. These were created by inserting a contrasting Bakelite color into a drilled hole. When comparing value with the same napkin ring style, rodded eyes increase the value of the piece.

Rabbits with "rodded" eyes $80-$100 each
Rabbits with no eyes $55-$75

Rabbits with painted tails $70-$90 each

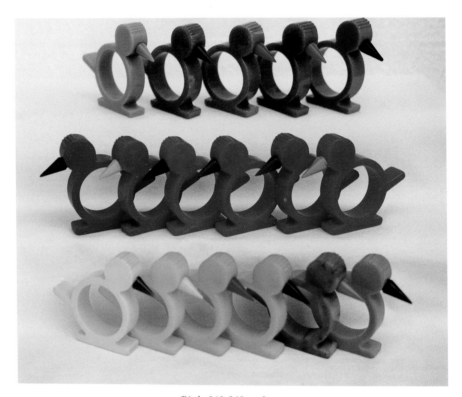

Birds $40-$60 each
Birds with "rodded" eyes $50-$70 each

Sitting dogs with "rodded" eyes $70-$90 each
Sitting dogs with painted eyes or no eyes $50-$70 each

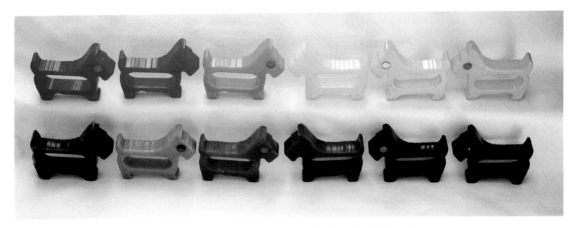

Standing Scotties with "rodded" eyes $65-$85 each
Standing Scotties with no eyes $45-$65 each

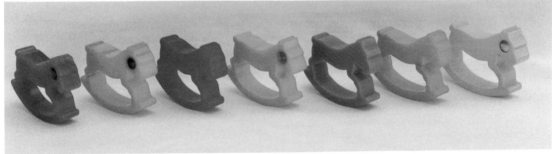

Rocking horses with "rodded eyes" $75-$95 each
Rocking horses with no eyes $65-$85 each

Ducks with "rodded" eyes $75-$95 each
Ducks with no eyes $65-$85 each

Fish with "rodded" eyes $70-$90 each
Fish with no eyes $45-$65 each

Roosters with "rodded" eyes $100-$120 each
Roosters with painted eyes or no eyes $80-$100 each

Skinny penguins with "rodded" eyes (none shown) $70-$90 each
Skinny penguins with no eyes $45-$65 each
Fat penguin (RARE!) $120-$140

Camel with "rodded" eyes $100-$120
Camel with no eyes $80-$100

Squirrel (Shown with Bakelite jewelry!) $80-$100

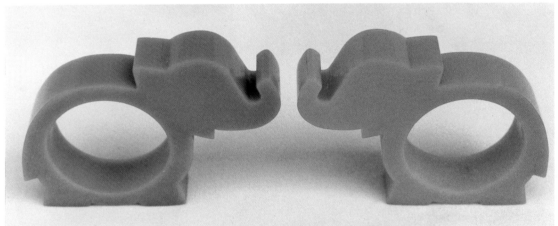

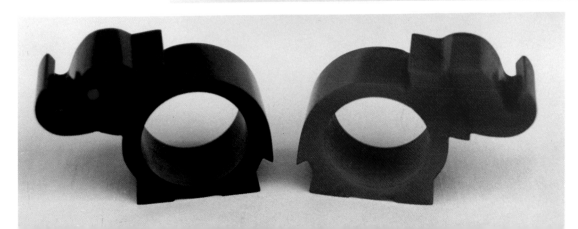

Elephants $80-$100 each

175

Elephant with red Bakelite ball in trunk (RARE!) $120-$140

This is a truly unique napkin ring. The cuts to create separate pieces have been made but are incomplete. An advanced collector would be willing to add this fascinating but not necessarily aesthetic piece to a display. $150-$175

Two-colored cat and dog napkin rings $150-$175 each

Mickey Mouse $150-$175 each

Donald Duck $150-$175

Popeye $150-$175

World's Fair $150-$175
This Napkin Ring is a "cross collectible"; that is, persons collecting World's Fair memorabilia can be as enthusiastic about it as Bakelite collectors.

Syrup Pitchers

Still popular today, syrup pitchers are readily found in a variety of handle styles and colors. Presented here is an abbreviated selection of the many possibilities.

This particular syrup pitcher stands 6.75 inches tall and has a black Bakelite handle on a lid patented in 1932. The blunt handle design of this piece is found in red, yellow, gold, and green Bakelite. Shown is the most elusive style/color combination of all worth $30-$40. Other blunt-handled syrups will cost $20-$35.

These syrup pitchers have the very popular bullet handles. Photographed are two distinctly different sizes, the red is 5 inches tall and the green is 9 inches tall, to provide examples of the size options available to collectors. Additional sizes in between these two are available. The lid was patented in 1939. $25-$50 depending on size, the larger the pitcher the higher the price.

The third main style of syrup pitchers is presented here. The advertisements from 1939 (*Country Gentleman* red print) and 1940 (*McCall's* blue print) indicate that it was available as a premium with the purchase of Karo Syrup. $30-$40

CHAPTER 4: WONDERFUL PIECES WORTHY OF CONSIDERATION

At the Bar

Here are a few exciting Bakelite pieces to enhance the bartender's efforts.

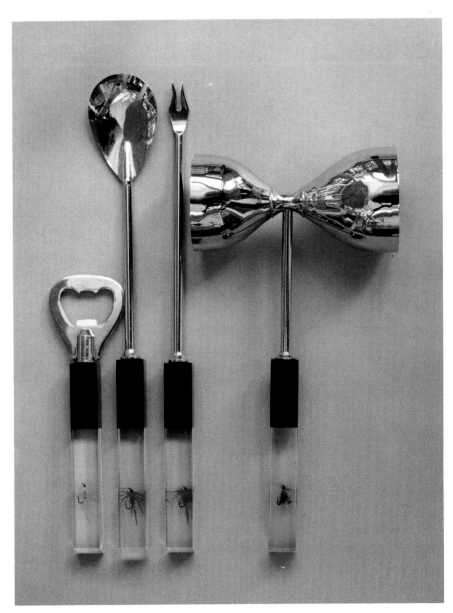

Four-piece Bakelite and Lucite Bar Set $75-$100

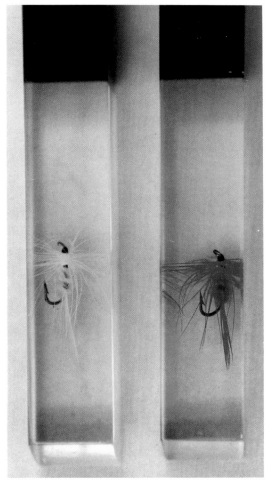

A close-up reveals the fishing flies that are imbedded in each handle.

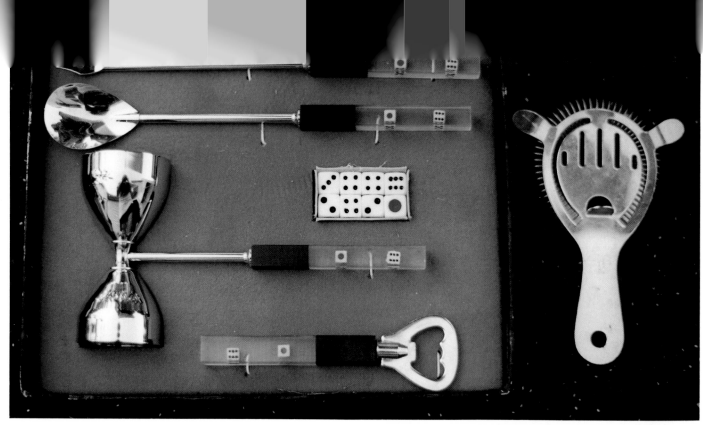

This five-piece Bar Set has dice in the Bakelite and Lucite handles.
Extra dice are provided! $75-$100

Drink mixers $30-$40 each

Drink mixers $40-
$50 each

Children's Utensils

One doesn't need a child to appreciate the magical splendor of these little pieces originally created for little people.

$30-$35 each

Knives are much more difficult to find than forks or spoons. For this reason they command a higher price. $35-$40

Fork $30-$35, knife $35-$40

Forks and spoons $30-$35 each, knife $35-$40
A complete set with a matching fork, knife, and spoon may cost more than three separate, unmatched pieces.

Fork and spoon $30-$35 each, knife $35-$40

Bakelite and Lucite $100-$110 per pair

Ornate handles $35-$40 each

Lucite, not Bakelite $30-35 each

Dogs in contrasting Bakelite inserted in handles $60-$70 each

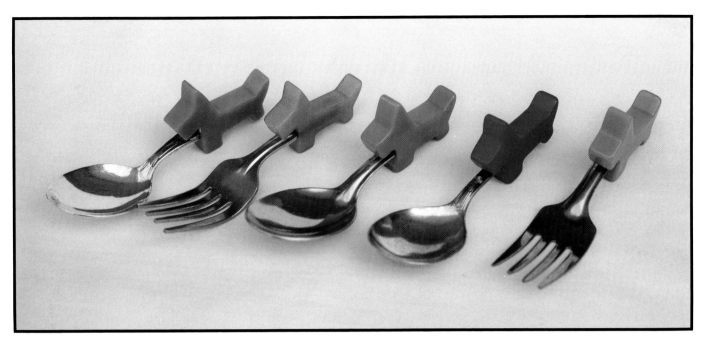

Scotty handles $50-$60 each

Cats in contrasting Bakelite inserted in handles $60-$70 each

Rabbits in contrasting Bakelite inserted in handles $70-$80 each

Careful buffing revealed the blue Bakelite that long ago had faded and darkened. $60-$70

Soldiers and geese in contrasting Bakelite inserted in handles $80-$90 each

Other Kitchen Pieces

In alphabetical order, here are some singular Bakelite treasures that should not be overlooked!

Brush: Stanley Home Products
Westfield Mass. U.S.A. 5.5 inches
long $18-$20

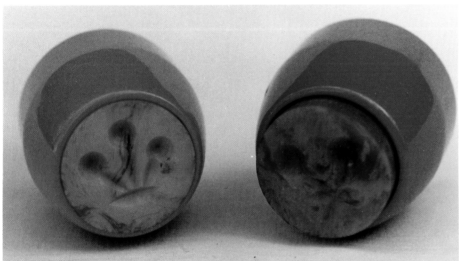

Two butter molds $75-$90 each

Two condiments with Bakelite lids and under plates $125-$150 each

Napkin holder decorated on one side. It is possible that this was part of three pieces that fit together. $85-$100

Small bird placecard holders $80-$100 each
Bird on pedestal placecard holder $100-$120

"Sectioner": In theory one would push down on the red Bakelite knob to core and separate the sections of a grapefruit. $85-$100

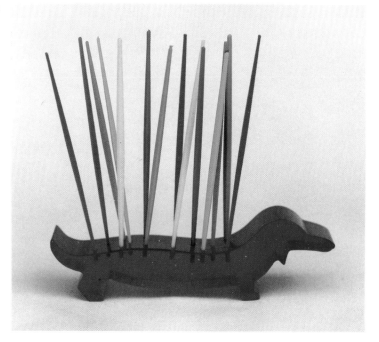

Lucite, not Bakelite, toothpick holder $75-$90

Some Final Treasures

In alphabetical order, here is a sampling of a few unique Bakelite offerings too fun to ignore!

4 inch tall bell with a Bakelite handle $25-$30

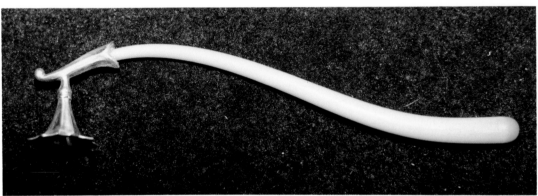

Aluminum candle snuffer with a Bakelite handle $70-$85

FLOWER-ANCHOR (frog) Specialty Guild Inc. Only 1 inch tall and 1.5 inches across $35-$40

Bates Flower Cutter 6.5 inches long $35-$40

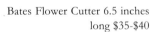

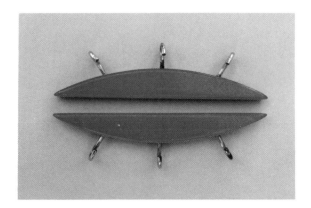

Pair of hooks on Bakelite bases 4.25 inches long. Two holes are in each unit to attach them to a cabinet, door, or wall. $35-$45 each

4.75 inch long KORN BARBER Made in Chicago for removing corns from one's foot. $20-$25

Nail file with an unusual swirl of gold and red-orange Bakelite. 7.5 inches long $25-$30

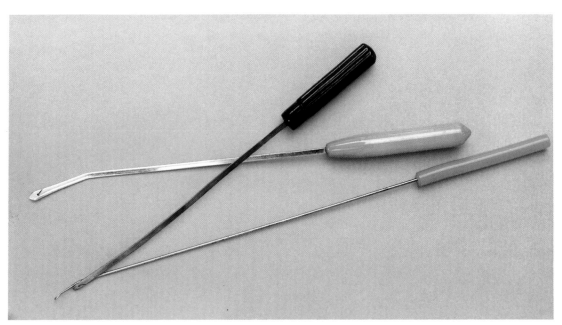

Three hooks for weaving. All are Federal Stainless Steel measuring from 8-9.75 inches. $20-$25 ea.

CHAPTER 5: RENEWING BAKELITE

Introduction

This process must be done in a well-ventilated location, and it is essential that a mask be worn. You will be creating dust that should not be ingested or breathed in. We recommend that you wear gloves and when you are done be sure to thoroughly wash your clothes and your hands.

Once you have had the opportunity to work on a variety of pieces this process becomes quite simple albeit time-consuming. Jim can spend as much as 40-60 minutes renewing one Bakelite and Lucite handle. He is also able to look at a dull, drab-colored piece of Bakelite and predict what the finished color(s) will be. Until you are fairly experienced we suggest that you start with damaged pieces. Look for cracked, burned, and otherwise "worthless" Bakelite that you would have discarded. Work through the process many, many times before attempting to renew a "keeper." Once you are comfortable and confident start with the *underside* of a utensil so if you make a mistake it will be hidden when you set the table. Experimentation and repeated practice is greatly recommended before you tackle a piece that you really treasure. These results can vary tremendously; one piece looking absolutely lovely and another taking on hues that are unexpected and possibly unwanted.

There are two basic processes used to renew Bakelite. The first is done through polishing. This technique is recommended for use on single-colored handles that have no scratching or only minor scratching. Successful polishing will enhance the Bakelite and create a lovely gloss and gleam. Swirls of color found in end-of-the-day Bakelite will have more a lively appearance after being polished. The second technique of renewing Bakelite is to refurbish it through a process of sanding followed by polishing. This is the method to select for handles of multiple colors. Renewing Bakelite through sanding will also produce color changes. For example, one can expect the following color transitions to occur if there is adequate sanding:

yellow turns to white
butterscotch turns to white
army green may turn to blue or dark green
black may turn to deep blue
orange may turn to pink
red may turn brighter

Surprises are to be expected, and these may be positive or negative. Occasionally a one-of-a-kind handle reveals an inlay of a color that was not apparent prior to sanding. **If you don't like uncertainty, don't sand your Bakelite! Laminated Bakelite cannot be buffed or sanded and should not be subjected to the following techniques.**

Polishing Bakelite

Tools:
Table-mounted grinder with two buffing wheels
Red rouge
White rouge
Dust mask
Gloves
Rags or paper towels
Goggles

Shown are the essential tools for renewing Bakelite: goggles,
dust mask, assorted sandpapers, red rouge, and white rouge.

Buffing wheels are made of layers of cloth that have been stitched together. You need to remove the outer 1/3 of the stitching that holds the layers together allowing the layers to separate and the wheels to become fluffier.

Reach in between the layers of the buffing wheel to cut the stitches.

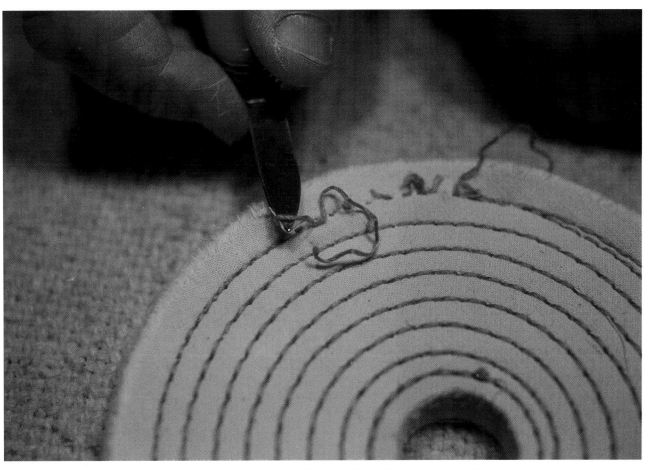

Remove the stitches of the buffing wheel by cutting along the outside.

This is what the buffing wheel will look like after removing one-third of the outer most stitches.

Basic Steps:

1. Wash
2. Red rouge buffing
3. Wipe
4. White rouge buffing
5. Wash

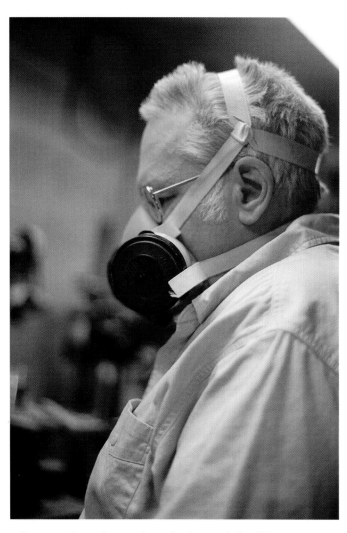

Jim wears glasses, but goggles and a dust mask should be worn during the entire process.

This red Bakelite handle has not been buffed.

Step 1: Select a piece of Bakelite that has no burn marks and is close to the color that you really want. Colors that are swirled or even are best. (Note: maroon Bakelite will not polish into a cherry red). Clean by wiping or wash with soap and water thus removing excess film and dirt.

Step 2: Prepare the buffing wheel with red rouge buffing compound. (Red rouge has a capability of removing fine scratches.) The cloth wheel should already have about 1/3 of the outermost stitches removed. Turn on the grinder and hold the rouge to the wheel for about 10-15 seconds. This will be enough rouge for about a dozen handles. Lightly buff the entire Bakelite handle by *constantly* turning while applying a light but even pressure. Do not allow heat to build up. If you do, stop and allow the Bakelite to cool. Minor warming is acceptable, but too much heat will cause the Bakelite to burn.

Lightly buff the entire Bakelite handle with red rouge by *constantly* turning while applying a light but even pressure. Do not allow heat to build up.

These buffing wheels have been used. Once a color is applied to a wheel it should not be changed. Here red rouge is always on the left and white rouge is always on the right.

Red rouge is being applied to the wheel.

White rouge is being applied to the other wheel.

Step 3: Wipe the handle with an old cloth or paper towel. Recheck for condition- look for minor surface scratches. If the scratches are shallow and very fine you can repeat Step 2.

Step 4: Prepare another buffing wheel with white rouge buffing compound. The cloth wheel should already have about 1/3 of the outermost stitches removed. Turn on the grinder and hold the rouge to the wheel for about 10-15 seconds. This will be enough rouge for about a dozen handles. Lightly buff the entire Bakelite handle by *constantly* turning while applying a light but even pressure. Do not allow heat to build up. If you do, stop and allow the Bakelite to cool. Minor warming is acceptable, but too much heat will cause the Bakelite to burn. This step is the one that creates the gloss and gleam.

Lightly buff the entire Bakelite handle with white rouge by *constantly* turning while applying a light but even pressure. Do not allow heat to build up.

Step 5: Wash taking time to remove excess buffing compound from crevices. Dry.

Step 6: Enjoy!

The buffing process is complete.

Refurbishing Bakelite

Tools:
Table-mounted grinder with two buffing wheels*
Red rouge
White rouge
Dust mask
Goggles
Gloves
Sandpaper: 6 varieties
Medium, fine, extra fine sandpaper 200, 400, 600 grit wet sandpaper
Small fine-toothed file and/or Exact-o knife

Container of water
Rags or paper towels

*buffing wheels are made of layers of cloth that have been stitched together. You need to remove the outer 1/3 of the stitching that holds the layers together allowing the layers to separate and the wheels to become fluffier.

Optional:
Dental tools
Small picks and files
Masking tape

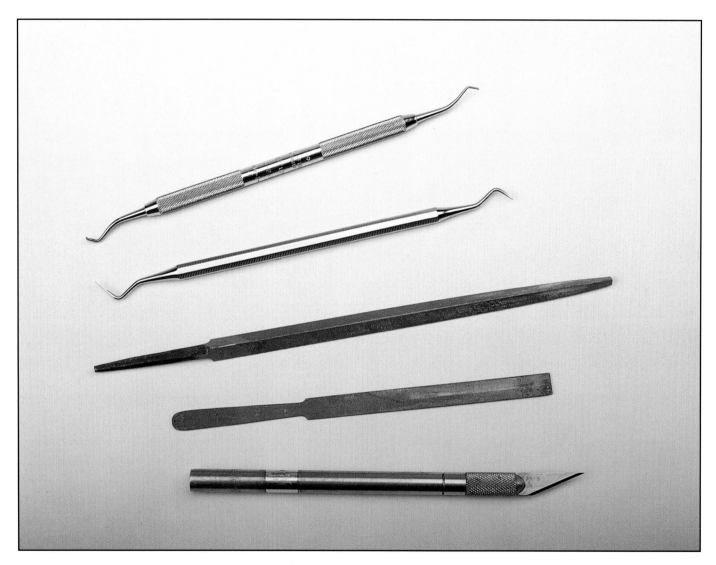

Shown are tools that simply make the job of renewing Bakelite a little easier: dental tools, small files, and an Exact-o knife.

Basic Steps:

1. Taping (optional)
2. Medium-grade sanding
3. Exact-o knife touch-up
4. Fine-grade sanding
5. Extra fine-grade sanding
6. 200 grit wet sanding
7. 400 grit wet sanding
8. 600 grit wet sanding
9. Red rouge buffing
10. Wipe
11. White rouge buffing
12. Wash

Step 1: This is an optional step that Jim does not do, however he recommends that until you become adept at handling sandpaper you take the time for this step. Cover all metal parts of the utensil with masking tape for protection from the sandpaper.

Step 2: Start sanding with coarsest sandpaper, which is a medium grade. If the utensil you selected has Bakelite and Lucite, concentrate on the Bakelite. Lucite responds much faster to sanding and will require very little sanding throughout the process. Sand lengthwise, that is along the length of the handle. Do not sand across the width. Continue to sand with this grade until the Bakelite reaches the desired color. It is important to watch the handle as you do this because you are removing material. Excessive sanding will cause the handle to become concave and can remove designs and textures.

Sand lengthwise, that is along the length of the handle, with the coarsest grade of sandpaper.

Step 3: Hold the item so the Bakelite is down and the metal is up and use a file or Exact-o knife to scrape the bit of Bakelite by the connector that may have been missed during the sanding process. Work at this until the colors match. Jim uses dental tools for this step.

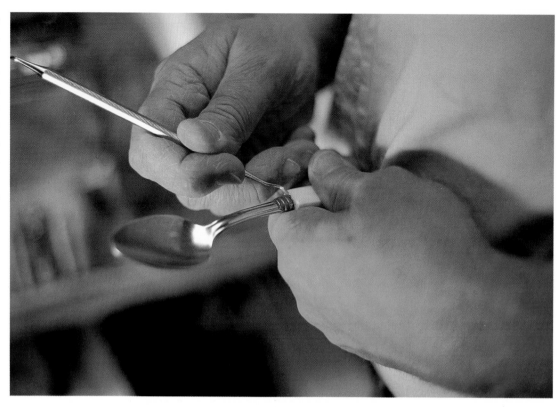

Use a file or Exact-o knife to scrape the bit of Bakelite by the connector that may have been missed during the sanding process.

Step 4: Using the fine grade sandpaper continue to sand in the lengthwise direction. This step begins the process of removing the scratching created in Step 2. From this point forward, each step of sanding is simply designed to reduce scratching. The initial sanding is to get the color, the others are to repair the scratching. The amount of time spent using this grade of paper is determined by the amount of scratching you need to remove. This is a trial and error process.

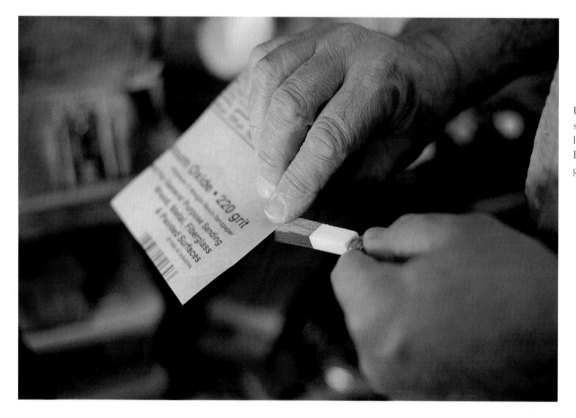

Use the fine grade sandpaper and sand in the lengthwise direction. Follow this with the finest grade sandpaper.

202

Step 5: Using the extra fine sandpaper again sand in the lengthwise direction until the scratches are further minimized.

This handle has had three levels of dry sandpaper and is ready for wet sandpaper.

Soak the 200 grit sandpaper in water for about ten seconds before sanding.

Step 6: Now switch to the wet sandpaper. Soak the 200 grit sandpaper in water for about ten seconds. Sand with the wet paper again in the lengthwise direction to further reduce scratches. Wash and dry the handle. Examine the results thus far looking for scratches versus smoothness. If the handle is looking rather smooth go on to the 400 and then the 600 grit wet sandpaper. If the handle is still fairly scratched continue with the 200 grit sandpaper. Jim rarely returns to dry sanding once the wet sanding has begun. The only reason to return to the dry sanding is if you are unhappy with the color results and want to remove more material.

Sand with the wet paper again in the lengthwise direction. This process of wet sanding continues with three grades of sandpaper.

Step 7: Soak the 400 grit sandpaper in water for about ten seconds. Sand with the wet paper again in the lengthwise direction to further reduce scratches.

Step 8: Soak the 600 grit sandpaper in water for about ten seconds. Sand with the wet paper again in the lengthwise direction to further reduce scratches. After completing sanding with the 200, 400, and 600 grit wet sandpaper, dry the entire piece.

Step 9: Prepare the buffing wheel with red rouge buffing compound. (Red rouge has a capability of removing fine scratches.) The cloth wheel should already have about 1/3 of the outermost stitches removed. Turn on the grinder and hold the rouge to the wheel for about 10-15 seconds. This will be enough rouge for about a dozen handles. Lightly buff the entire Bakelite handle by *constantly* turning while applying a light but even pressure. Do not allow heat to build up. If you do, stop and allow the Bakelite to cool. Minor warming is acceptable, but too much heat will cause the Bakelite to burn.

After preparing the buffing wheel with red rouge lightly buff the entire Bakelite handle by *constantly* turning while applying a light but even pressure.

Step 10: Wipe the handle with an old cloth or paper towel. Recheck for condition- look for minor surface scratches. If the scratches are shallow and very fine you can repeat the wet sanding using the 400 and then the 600 grit wet sandpaper. Then repeat Step 9.

Step 11: Prepare another buffing wheel with white rouge buffing compound. The cloth wheel should already have about 1/3 of the outermost stitches removed. Turn on the grinder and hold the rouge to the wheel for about 10-15 seconds. This will be enough rouge for about a dozen handles. Lightly buff the entire Bakelite handle by *constantly* turning while applying a light but even pressure. Do not allow heat to build up. If you do, stop and allow the Bakelite to cool. Minor warming is acceptable, but too much heat will cause the Bakelite to burn. This step is the one that creates the gloss and gleam.

After preparing the buffing wheel with white rouge lightly buff the entire Bakelite   handle by *constantly* turning while applying a light but even pressure.

Step 12: Wash taking time to remove excess buffing compound from crevices. Dry.

Step 13: Enjoy!

These two salad forks are identical however the one on the bottom has been sanded and buffed making the "butterscotch" Bakelite lighten to near-white and the blue Lucite much more transparent.

These two knives are identical however the one on the top has been sanded and buffed.

Each of these knives began as an army green handle with a butter-scotch chevron. After completing the renewing process one revealed a green Bakelite handle and the other a blue Bakelite handle.

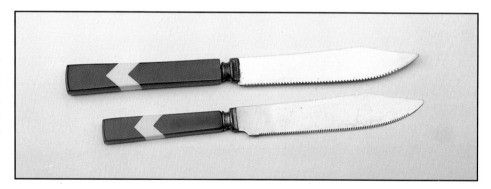

This child's fork started as an army green handle with a butterscotch cat. After sanding and buffing the handle became a lovely blue and white.

The four-piece place setting was originally dark red and butterscotch. The renewing process lightened the Lucite and made it completely transparent. The butterscotch Bakelite is now virtually white.

Shown are three Bakelite and Lucite handles in various color combinations. All have been sanded and buffed.

Two chevron soup spoons have been renewed. The top handle is entirely Bakelite and the bottom is a unique combination of Bakelite and Lucite.

This iced tea spoon began as a brown handle. Sanding revealed the uncommon light blue with white Bakelite.

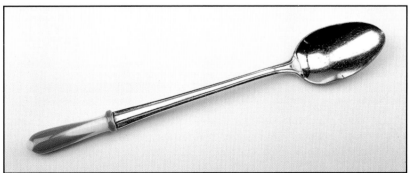

ENDNOTES

[1] Howard, *Table Ways of Today*.(U.S.A.: Oneida Community, Ltd., 1930): p.10.
[2] Ibid.

BIBLIOGRAPHY

Howard, Kathleen et al. *Table Ways of Toady*. U.S.A.: Oneida Community, Ltd., 1930.

Mumford, John Kimberly. *The Story of Bakelite*. New York: Robert L. Stillson Company, 1924.

Wassertrom, Donna and Leslie Piña. *Bakelite Jewelry: good better best*. Atglen, Pennsylvania: Schiffer Publishing Ltd., 1997.